What people are saying about

Meaning Indicator

This timely and compelling book is a must-read for anyone seeking to leave a meaningful imprint on our world. Full of wise counsel, meaningful reflection exercises, and stories of real people, including the author, *Meaning Indicator* will guide your journey and inspire your heart and soul.

Lisa Lahey, EdD, Harvard Graduate School of Education, co-founder of Minds at Work, author of *Immunity to Change* and *An Everyone Culture*

We are seeing a rise in greater-good values in organizations and the emerging generation of leaders. An important read for anyone who is seeking to lead with a strong sense of purpose and meaning.

Carolyn Taylor, one of the world's foremost experts in organizational culture and the Executive Chair of Walking the Talk, author of long-time bestseller *Walking the Talk: Building a Culture Success* and *Accountability@Work*

Michelle's approach to finding purpose and meaning is different; it's grounded and practical. Her coaching backstory, with its roots in the Mormon church, grabs you while her simple, straightforward writing style propels you amiably but insistently through one rewarding chapter after another. There isn't a better or more important business read out there today.

Carlos Valdes-Dapena, formerly Director and Sr. Consultant, Change and Collaboration, Mars. Inc., and author of *Lessons from Mars: How One Global Company Cracked the Code on High Performance Collaboration and Teamwork* and *Virtual Teams: Holding the Center When You Can't Meet Face-to-Face*

Through her expertise in transformational change and grounded in wisdom, Michelle Hollingshead establishes a practical and accessible approach to experiencing meaning and significance in life and business. *Meaning Indicator* illustrates how profound change is possible with a practiced path.

Shauna Shapiro, PhD, professor, clinical psychologist, and internationally recognized expert in mindfulness and self-compassion, as well as author of *Good Morning, I Love You*; her TEDx, The Power of Mindfulness, has been viewed over three million times

Michelle Hollingshead has written a useful and practical book. Synthesizing past wisdom, writings, and theories, she introduces approachable ways to create meaning and purpose in our lives. Through sharing her personal stories, Hollingshead encourages readers to think deeply, to learn from and discover meaning from all of life's circumstances.

Patrick Williams, EdD, MCC, former board member of the International Coach Federation (ICF), inaugural member of the ICF's Circle of Distinction, and founding member of Harvard University's Institute of Coaching; author of *Becoming a Professional Life Coach: The Art and Science of a Whole-Person Approach*

Michelle Hollingshead shines a light on the fundamental source that knocks us off center or takes us out. She communicates a timely and needed message for all humans with simple but not necessarily easy antidotes.

Fran Fisher, MCC, internationally recognized as one of the pioneers of the coaching profession, founding executive board member of the International Coach Federation, recipient of the ICF 2022 Circle of Distinction Award

Meaning Indicator

Finding Significance through
Challenge, Work, and Love

Meaning Indicator

Finding Significance through
Challenge, Work, and Love

Michelle Hollingshead

CHANGEMAKERS
BOOKS

Winchester, UK
Washington, USA

JOHN HUNT PUBLISHING

First published by Changemakers Books, 2024
Changemakers Books is an imprint of John Hunt Publishing Ltd., No. 3 East Street,
Alresford, Hampshire SO24 9EE, UK
office@jhpbooks.com
www.johnhuntpublishing.com
www.changemakers-books.com

For distributor details and how to order please visit the 'Ordering' section on our website.

ISBN: 978 1 80341 513 0
978 1 80341 546 8 (ebook)
Library of Congress Control Number: 2023935622

A CIP catalogue record for this book is available from the British Library.

Design: Lapiz Digital Services

UK: Printed and bound by CPI Group (UK) Ltd, Croydon, CR0 4YY
Printed in North America by CPI GPS partners

We operate a distinctive and ethical publishing philosophy in
all areas of our business, from our global network of authors to
production and worldwide distribution.

Contents

For Addison and Jack

Life is ten thousand joys and ten thousand sorrows.
A Zen saying

Acknowledgments

I am extremely grateful to the many people who helped bring *Meaning Indicator* to fruition. Thank you to my first coach, Deborah Roth. Teri Carter, you helped me source the courage to write and reminded me I get to choose what writing I share with others. I am indebted to Deb Valle and Karen Boskemper, who were the catalysts for the first meaning interviews. Anne Dean Dotson, thank you for walking alongside me for the entirety of the project (especially when it got messy), helping me hone my voice and being a brilliant editor, writing coach, and dear friend. Rachel Marston, my sister, for our writing retreats by the lake and for your ceaseless thought partnership, kindness, and our silliness. I appreciate Nancy Barnett and Michael Potapov offering us your lake house and encouraging me to say Yes! Liz Sheehan, I am grateful for your expertise and different way of thinking that sharpened mine. Meghan Stone, you worked alongside me, coding all interviews and generating the protocol, and making it fun. To Jess Dobbins for your generosity and guidance in integrating the reader feedback. To Stevie Morrison for the graphic designs. To all the participants in the meaning interviews for entrusting me with your most precious stories and giving your permission to share them. For Whitney Collins, who helped me believe I would find a publisher. For Nick Kettles, who suggested I check out John Hunt Publishing, and Tim Ward at Changemakers, who wisely reminded me it will be useful for some. Thank you to all my partners in purpose and the global communities where I have grown and served: Axialent, ACT Leadership, Walking the Talk, CTI Bisons, Deep Mastery Wisdom Circle, and Subtle Power Yogis.

I am most grateful for the love and support of my husband, Dan, my daughter, Addison, and my son, Jack. For all the times we wrote our intentions and family possibilities, and for teaching me life is messy and perfect. And celebrating all their goodness and the gift of life, I am grateful for my parents, Debbie Lowell and the late Richard Marston.

Prologue

In my mid-twenties, I was unexpectedly excommunicated from the Mormon faith when I chose not to attend the Church court. Twelve men in suits waited to question me about my assumed sins, but I never showed up. Three weeks following my absence, I received a letter announcing the court's decision to excommunicate me.

Up to that moment, my religion had taught me how to be in a relationship with myself, others, and God. And now, it was no longer mine. Even though I had been moving away from Mormonism for some time, and exploring other faiths, philosophies, and world views, I didn't realize how much shame I would feel about this rejection. As I struggled to understand who I was, and how to create a path forward, I began a soul-searching journey.

Who would I become?

Shortly after my excommunication, my fiancé and I relocated from Las Vegas to Kentucky. With the move, I drew a clear line in my mind and decided not to look back. It was a fresh start in a new city where no one knew me as a Mormon. I consciously chose not to reveal this part of my story except with very close friends. I found it difficult to discuss my time in Spain, where I had served a mission for the Mormon Church. Instead of telling the truth, I described that time in my life under the umbrella of "humanitarian mission work" or "studying abroad."

I decided I would try to find a way to live a meaningful and fulfilling life on my terms. I spent the next two decades seeking ways to live a spiritual existence without a formal religious community. I explored different religions and philosophies. I took up therapy, marathon running, yoga, and mindfulness. Ultimately, I hired a professional coach to support me through a major life-career transition, and it was soon after that I decided to enroll in a coach training program to earn my coaching certification. In 2009, I founded my company, Imprint, with a mission to help individuals and organizations leave a meaningful imprint on our world.

On my new career path, I listened to many successful individuals across the globe, and discovered a large portion of humanity was struggling with burnout, loneliness, and disconnect from meaning and purpose in their lives and work. It echoed some of my own struggles, as well as my husband's, who had been dissatisfied with his job, despite being a top-level executive. I began to see that even with external accolades of success, many of us were without a sense of meaningfulness.

I began looking for ways to expand the definition of success and explored what a meaningful life could look and feel like in modern society. While reading Viktor Frankl's work *Man's Search for Meaning* (1946), I came upon the following words of wisdom, "Don't aim at success—the more you aim at it and make it a target, the more you are going to miss it. For success, like happiness, cannot be pursued: it must ensue, and it does so as the unintended side-effect of one's dedication to a cause greater than oneself." Frankl's words struck a deep chord in me, and moving forward I began to see that those who were most deeply satisfied with life were those individuals dedicated to something larger than their own self-interests. Those were the humans who were experiencing a deeper sense of joy, fulfillment, and ultimately success.

At the same time, I also began doing profound internal work and writing extensively about my excommunication. As I listened to stories about Mormon culture, I felt an invitation to revisit my roots and explore this part of my life I had set aside. During this personal process, I began to observe and listen to my clients with greater intention and launched a Meaning Research Project. Soon, I learned there were four main ways to define meaning—Comprehension, Purpose, Significance, and

Belonging. Furthermore, I hypothesized that there were three main ways people infused their experiences with meaning and found significance, and these were through: Work, Love, and Challenge. Work primarily entailed contributing to society; Love involved caring for self, others, and our world; and Challenge (with a sub-theme of Aspiration) focused on choosing courage during difficulty.

Equipped with these three indicators, and with the support of my sister, Rachel Marston, Ph.D., at St. John's University, I designed a process to interview individuals where I prompted them to describe three meaningful life experiences with the aim of determining which of the three ways resonated most. Which stories would people choose when asked to narrow to three? What path would bring them the most meaning? Did they gravitate toward Work, Love, or Challenge?

Next, I engaged Ph.D. Psychologist and Researcher Liz Sheehan at the University of Kentucky. Under her guidance, we coded each interview and generated a protocol to categorize each participant's shared experience as Work, Love, Challenge (Aspiration). We used the language from the developed protocol to create the line items for a quantitative scale.

Simultaneously, we conducted a literature search and found 20 existing instruments that measured meaning in life, as well as other facets. We examined the line items and findings from this research conducted between 1964 and 2018 to understand how others assessed meaning in life. Five of these scales measured purpose in life, four measured meaning in life, three measured life attitude, and the others assessed things like the effect of mood on meaning, a person's tendency toward boredom in life, and life satisfaction.

We launched the pilot study and gathered data to test my hypothesis and the categories. I interviewed 30 people, the recommended initial sample size for qualitative research, and invited these same people to participate in a quantitative questionnaire. The end result is this book, *Meaning Indicator*. Throughout it, I share parts of my personal story and the ideas that helped shape my approach to understanding my life events, choices, and how I find significance. I also share the stories told by the interviewees and have chosen to preserve the language they used to describe their culture, values, race, identity, and experiences. Only one participant requested to have their name changed. But above all, I provide a fresh way to define meaning through the four dimensions of Comprehension, Purpose, Significance, and Belonging, and a way to experience it through Challenge, Work, and Love.

It is my hope that this book finds you at the right moment. Whether you are facing a challenge much greater than you believe you can navigate or are experiencing grief, exhaustion, or simply questioning life's purpose, I hope the *Meaning Indicator* reminds you to keep going and that the stories inspire your heart and soul. The experiences and practices offered within, can be utilized to both restore hope and empower. In the words of Francois Jacob, "It is hope that gives life meaning. And hope is based on the prospect of being able one day to turn the actual world into a possible one that looks better."

—Michelle

Chapter 1

Comprehension

The meaning is in the mess.
Anne Dean Dotson

Why Meaning Matters, and Why Now?

Comprehension is how we make sense of our lives. It is the narrative we construct to understand who we are. I believe we are, currently and collectively, in a crisis for meaning. As human beings, we want to feel significant. We crave for others to accept us. Because of this, we pick up on the messages we receive about what is valued, and we tend to adapt our behavior to fit in. For the majority of us, this happens unconsciously and it shapes our identities. It usually works for a while, and then, at some point, most of us will tire of this and consider the question: *Who am I?* It is my belief that we can find the answer to this question, and move from crisis to significance, through telling our stories, exploring what motivates our choices and goals, and contemplating what makes life worth living.

That said, we all tell our stories differently. We create narratives around who matters and who doesn't, and it's no surprise that our collective identity is in upheaval right now. More people are sharing their stories, and many of these stories challenge long-held beliefs, assumptions, and biases. Psychologist Erik Erikson defines an identity crisis as a time of intensive analysis and exploration of looking at oneself.[1] This is occurring on a personal level, as well as a collective level. And it feels a little messy. It may help to take a look at the human condition and a few of our paradoxes to better understand what is at play.

For starters, research on well-being has shown that human beings have experienced an overall increase in wealth and prosperity, decreased poverty, and increased longevity. Research has also shown that there is no increase in happiness, joy, or well-being beyond a certain level of material prosperity. And yet, despite this knowledge, we continue to have a significant income and wealth gap in America. Culturally, we celebrate the accumulation of more, and we call this success.

With the accessibility of technology and social media, many assume we would feel more connected. We can track our kids through their phones, we have the presence of influencers and seemingly "perfect" families, and our friends post whatever they want us to see. Yet, in the United States, we report greater hopelessness, loneliness, anxiety, depression, and suicide. Many studies cite that the mental health risks for teens and young adults have worsened since the beginning of this century.[2]

In addition, since the late 2000s, depression rates among children have increased. When researchers analyzed the data on suicides and attempted suicides, the same trends held. Rates of suicidal thoughts, plans, and attempts all elevated as well. While other countries have seen suicide rates fall, the US has seen rates increase more sharply.[3] We clearly also feel more isolated despite being more "connected" than ever.

On top of these trends, there is a shift in the religious landscape in the United States. When asked about their religion, fewer American adults describe themselves as a part of a particular denomination, and religiously unaffiliated populations are increasing.[4] As religious constructs and narratives loosen, where are people finding moral community and seeking answers to ultimate questions?

All said, we are in a unique moment in history. We are expanding the reach of our voices through social networks, and we are disrupting our current economic, political, ecological, and cultural systems. We are grappling with the spread of disinformation, conspiracy theories, and polarization. There is the ongoing public health crisis of COVID-19 and its effects. Not to mention that during societal upheaval, humanity typically moves toward a collective desire for stabilization, opening a door for autocrats to seize power and take control. We are seeing this play out. How will we choose to make sense of what is happening and who we are becoming?

With an identity crisis comes the possibility for a new path forward. Despite so many struggles, so much of humanity is mobilized in serving the well-being of others. Individuals are reminding each other to take only what they need. Healthcare workers are risking their lives to care for others. Crucial conversations are happening about sexual violence and racial justice. People are asking themselves what really matters.

Finding significance can be an antidote to crisis. It can shift our perspective, transcending "the trivial or momentary" conditions of life to considering something larger.[5] Recent research has found a strong connection between mattering and deciding whether life is meaningful or not. Whether we view life in a spiritual sense (i.e., by being God's creation) or secular sense (i.e., by mattering to others or future generations), it impacts overall meaningfulness.[6] Experiencing life as meaningful has been linked to benefits such as healthier eating, more physical activity, higher life satisfaction, and lower depression.[7] When you feel like you matter, you feel like your actions make a difference and that life is worth living.

What Is Meaning in Life?

Meaning comes from the Old High German word *meinen*, which is related to the human mind's unique capacity for reflective and linguistic thinking. A meaningful life is characterized by four dimensions: Comprehension, Purpose, Significance, and Belonging.[8]

7

Dimensions of Meaning

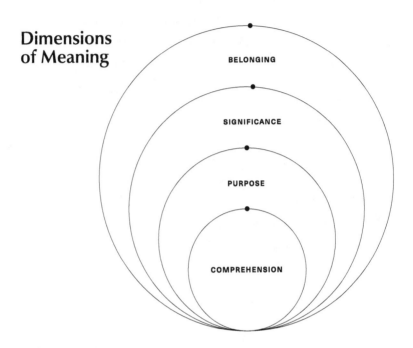

BELONGING

Belonging is being part of something greater than yourself.

SIGNIFICANCE

Significance is having a life worth living and a feeling your life matters.

PURPOSE

Purpose is a self-organizing life aim or direction. It shapes how you establish your story and reveals what motivates you.

COMPREHENSION

Comprehension is making sense of your life. It is the narrative you construct to understand who you are.

Many disciplines—including theology, religion, philosophy, and psychology—explore the concept of meaning. These are the dimensions recognized by positive psychology. Most research on meaning has centered around Comprehension and Purpose.

There is an important distinction between meaning as comprehension and sense-making and meaning as significance.

To find significance, you evaluate what makes life worth living and what makes you feel like your life matters. As recently as 2020, studies measuring mattering have emerged and early findings are encouraging. The results support focusing on understanding how people develop and maintain a sense of mattering in their lives.[9]

Each dimension of meaning offers questions for contemplation.

Questions for Contemplating Meaning in Life

Comprehension: *What happened to make me who I am? Who am I?*

Purpose: *How do I direct my life? What gives me a sense of purpose?*

Significance: *What makes life worth living? What makes me feel like my life matters?*

Belonging: *What can I give? How can I accompany others to find greater significance?*

What Happened to Make Me Who I Am?

For my personal story to make sense, it is crucial to understand what I longed for most: a happy family. In Mormonism, a happy family is mecca. The whole religious narrative revolves around eternal families, and from as early as I can remember, this dream was what I craved—partly because of my religious upbringing and partly because I was a child of divorce.

In addition, I was taught I needed a man to enter heaven. In the Mormon religion, men are granted a higher authority and easier access to God. For women, the focus was on being virtuous. I was taught that if I upheld my moral end of the bargain, I would attract a righteous man and get married in the Mormon temple, securing my dream of a happy, eternal family.

So, for the majority of my youth, I attended Mormon seminary each morning before high school and studied scripture—including the Old Testament, the New Testament, the Book of Mormon, and Pearl of Great Price—all in the hopes of achieving my dream. It was not until my early thirties, as I struggled with grief and overall lack of fulfillment that I began to seek a deeper understanding of myself. My original dream of a happy family was still important, but there was more to the picture now. As part of coaching, I looked at my life history differently. I started to explore my own needs, values, and beliefs. I thought about what I wanted to give. I thought about my desire to offer something meaningful.

Who Am I?

My perspective changed drastically after September 2001. The United States was in deep mourning. We spent hours each night glued to the news watching stories of families who lost loved ones during the attack. I cried. My heart was broken. I couldn't imagine how it felt to lose a loved one. Then ten days after 9/11, I received a call from my husband, Dan.

I was at my job at the time, teaching at a public elementary school, when I picked up the phone. Dan told me my younger brother, Matt, had passed away earlier that morning. It was just three days after his twenty-seventh birthday. I couldn't believe it. We flew back home to Las Vegas to say goodbye and bury Matt. I remember walking through the Chicago airport on our layover. It felt like a ghost town, eerily empty and without life. It felt like a foreshadowing of what I would experience when visiting my brother lying in his casket embalmed and in his best suit. How could this have happened? He was so young, and it seemed incredibly unfair.

Before this experience, I valued achieving my goals—my plans were at the top of my list. Suddenly, I woke up to the reality that there were many things in life I could not control. I faced the truth that life could and would change in an instant. Between 9/11 and Matt's death, I began wondering how people went on in the face of disaster and devastation. How could they still find joy and pleasure?

To manage my grief and anger, I began journaling about my feelings. It was difficult to watch my mom, who had such a resilient spirit, struggle to cope with the loss of her only son. During my grieving process for Matt, I realized I longed for something more in my life. I wanted to live life to the fullest and, as Thoreau says, "suck the marrow out of life." This wisdom is engraved on Matt's tombstone. For me, this didn't mean retreating from the world; it meant finding a way to contribute more authentically. I aspired to take more risks, understand myself and the mysteries of my life experiences—and make a difference in our world.

One of the most powerful works on meaning is *Man's Search for Meaning* (1946) by Viktor Frankl. He survived the Nazi concentration camps and created Logotherapy. Frankl believed the primary driving motivator was to find a purpose in life. He also believed that attitude—the way we choose to manage our mind, thoughts, and choices in response to any circumstance— is the last of the human freedoms. He lost his family during the Holocaust, and he understood the necessity to choose the most optimal response to his tragedy: to go on living and not give up. This wasn't a dismissal of the reality and terror of his pain and experience. It was a deep acceptance of what he was suffering. He could still be of service despite his extreme loss and witnessing the worst of humanity.

Through his experience, Frankl shaped his ideas, including being in control of your attitude or mindset, creating meaning, understanding your potential is waiting, and giving yourself to something greater than yourself. When we can connect our actions with a deeper sense of meaning and purpose, it inspires and motivates us to keep going in the face of difficulty. We each have the ultimate responsibility to choose how to respond to life's challenges and determine what we will give to the world. This is how we will create a meaningful life.

Your Potential Is Waiting

How can you remain present during life's hardest challenges? Can you be with whatever arises? Can you endure this suffering you experience and discover what wants to emerge from the darkness?

How do you intentionally create meaning even in the most dire of circumstances? Your potential is waiting to respond while bearing the tense struggle of detecting meaning. Make an inner commitment to your authentic self and choose to give something to the world worthy of your potential.

Human potential is realized through mastering this tension of opposites. This is an ancient concept from Chinese philosophy known as Yin and Yang. We find it in other traditions as well. There are two sides to everything, and we are often tempted to focus on only one polarity. A polarity is a pair of interdependent positive opposites. Both sides are strengths or values needed over time, though, for a healthy self or system. They help us live in balance.

We do not have a choice about opposites. We function and exist because of them. Think of your breath as an example. The breath exists of both the inhale and the exhale. We create our lives through this range of oppositional energies put in motion by our beliefs, attitudes, and emotions. How we choose to think, act, and relate to others matters and vice versa. We are part of a larger relationship system and collective consciousness.

Who Do We Want to Be?

In a crisis for meaning, we have the opportunity to consider these existential questions collectively. *What happened to make me who I am? Who am I?* It takes great courage to explore our history and contradictions, to let our story move on, to allow a new version of ourselves. Who do we want to be?

Generativity is the concern in establishing and guiding the next generation. In other words, your life matters for something beyond the self. Costin and Vignoles suggest, "Highly generative individuals are more likely to construct stories that involve awareness of the suffering of others, redeeming bad situations into good outcomes, and committing to goals that benefit others."[10]

How we construct our new story matters.

Something that connects us is our perspective, our lens. We view the world through a lens shaped by our experiences, beliefs, and values. This is how we make sense of who we are and tell our story. This also includes our biases which are usually hidden from us.

Our way of looking or thinking about something impacts how we choose to perceive or ignore what is happening around us. If we allow it, disruptions and disorienting life events can be catalysts for deeper contemplation. They shift our perspective of who we are and our potential. This is what happened when I was excommunicated from the Mormon church and lost my brother Matt. My lens widened.

Globally and collectively, our lens is widening. I believe this is our opportunity to look with curiosity and compassion at the perspectives shaping our narratives. To consider the suffering of others. To redeem bad situations into good outcomes. To commit to goals that benefit others. To generate a better future from the mess.

Chapter 2

Purpose

The meaning of life is to find your gift. The purpose of life is to give it away.
Pablo Picasso

One of the simplest ways to bring meaning into our lives, is to define what feels purposeful to us. We can open our minds, hearts, and will to something larger than ourselves, especially following disorienting life events. I believe these events are an invitation to give significant thought to what you want your life to be about. From this awareness, you can start making choices so your life reflects the answer. This sense of purpose reorients you to your potential.

Having a sense of purpose asks you to adopt a larger vision of who you are and clarify how you want to direct your life energy. Purpose deepens when you shift from a singular focus to a more global reach of how you could influence the world for the better. What can you give?

Now What?

Something had gone off track, but I did not know where. I realized the life I had created was not the life I wanted anymore. From all external markers of success, my husband and I had achieved the traditional American Dream, the one from a 1950's sitcom. My husband had a successful career. I stayed at home with the children and took them to their playgroups. Our house was in a picture-perfect neighborhood.

And yet, this life was how I was slowly going numb. It appeared to check all the boxes, but beneath the checklist, I was feeling dissatisfied and disconnected. I had created the life my younger self so desperately wanted, and yet it felt suffocating. Dan traveled most weeks for work and was exhausted. I felt angry and overwhelmed. I was still grieving my brother Matt. Deep down, I was yearning for something more, but there was little time for meaningful connection, with myself or others. Eventually, Dan and I decided to spend a night away to find some space for our relationship. We started to talk about our dreams and the life we each *really* desired. Dan revealed that he actually hated his job and would quit tomorrow if he could. I admitted I was miserable, too, and wanted to make some changes. We returned home with a flicker of hope. Our honesty with ourselves and one another had set something in motion.

When you speak your truth, things move. I could feel an air of possibility coming back. We decided to get help. We hired a marriage and family therapist, and soon after, I hired my coach. I began to experience a renewed sense of self and creative potential. I believed we could make a change.

How Do I Direct My Life?

The key to living the life and doing the work you love is living true to the essence of who you are—I mean who you really are at the core of your being.
Fran Fisher

An open heart meets life's mysteries and disorienting events with humility and reverence. It takes courage and resolve to stay open when you do not yet understand what needs to happen. It is important to remain curious about what draws you. Try to feel your potential even in the midst of suffering and uncertainty. Try paying attention to what is happening in the field of your existence, no matter how challenging.

For me, this means trusting in my personal vision for my life, in maintaining my interests and goals, in staying true to who I want to be. It also means being willing to admit when something isn't working any longer and being brave enough to take steps to explore change. Connecting our thinking and actions with a sense of purpose inspires and motivates us to persevere and recover from negative emotions more quickly.[1]

When Dan and I decided to take a risk and start our own businesses, it was an exhilarating and scary time. We had two young children, and we were in the middle of the Great Recession. We had so much to lose and so much to gain. To manage my stress levels, I began practicing yoga and mindfulness. Dan and I began to live more intentionally and in the present moment.

Who would you like to be?

Take a moment to reflect on who you would like to be.[2] What characteristics and attributes do you want to embody?

If you are stuck, a mind map, like you used in English class, can be a fun way to get your receptivity flowing.

What Gives Me a Sense of Purpose?

I am a life-long learner and teacher. What gives me a sense of purpose is easing suffering and raising consciousness—mine and ours. I like having conversations that generate awareness and provoke new ways of thinking and talking about things. With awareness comes choice. If you are facing a transition or loss, like I was, pointing your life toward something bigger than the problems you currently face can elevate your growth and healing.

I believe purpose helps answer how your potential can serve humanity. Being curious about how that evolves is more important than having a crafted statement you don't really remember. Most of the time, this purpose or mission statement doesn't come so much from what you know. It comes from what you don't know, are reaching for, or are missing.

Life purpose does not come easy to most of us. It doesn't easily fit into one word, category, or neat statement. So how do you pay attention to it? And how do you connect with it?

Your life energy has an organizing aim. It is the heartbeat. You don't have to tell your heart to pump. Similarly, there is the part of you that knows and moves into the unknown sensing what you are attracted to and curious about. You don't call it purpose when you are in the experience; you simply move with it and from it. Even if you don't name it, it is still there. It is a movement with intelligence and resonance from the heart. You feel it.

Making a Life and a Living

Having a sense of purpose can help orient your motivation at work. For some, it might be that finding meaningful work is not as important as long as your work allows you the time and freedom to pursue what is most meaningful to you outside of work. You can find peace in recognizing and appreciating your career for financial support.

For others, work is a way to realize your potential through your contributions. When you are aligned with your values and using your strengths and natural gifts, you will most likely make the most meaningful contribution. Even if you believe your offering is small, it can impact others positively.

There are three main motivation theories: instinctual, extrinsic, and intrinsic. The earliest motivation theory is instinctual motivation. It's the belief that motivation is primarily biologically based. For a behavior to be an instinct, it must be a pattern in a species and be unlearned. For example, babies have a rooting reflex that is innate and occurs in all infants.

Extrinsic motivation theory is goals-based and relies on the carrot-and-stick reward model. People do certain things, such as getting good grades, to realize a desired reward like getting into their preferred college. Or they do other things to avoid an undesirable consequence or punishment, such as failing and not getting into their top school. This particular theory operates under the assumption that social status and external markers of success motivate people.

Intrinsic motivation theory is values-based and emphasizes the values a person self-authors versus what they adopt from their culture or environment to fit in and succeed. I once coached a business leader who left a very lucrative position at a well-known company because the business was no longer making decisions aligned with his values. They asked him to do things he didn't agree with. He came to realize he was willing to make less money in exchange for working in a way that honored his values. Our driving motivations vary throughout life and evolve as we increase in understanding and awareness of ourselves.

Most of us feel this tension between our needs and values. We have basic needs that are driving motivators. We need to make a living, but we also want to make a life that feels worth living. More often than not, needs will find a way to get met; they are not optional. When I was starting my business, I had financial needs to consider as well as emotional. When we are aware of our needs, and act responsibly to get them met in constructive ways, we can spend more energy living from our values. Values determine who you are, what you want, and how you live your life.

Many are undertaking this inner journey or process of self-actualization earlier in life and questioning how they define success. This requires overcoming fear and is much more difficult than simply running around to pursue material gratifications. I believe we are experiencing this with the pandemic and what we are calling the Great Resignation.

What Could Success Look Like?

Depletion of human beings over time shows up in society as dis-ease, dis-satisfaction, dis-connection from self and others. It manifests as depression, despair, helplessness, and anxiety. In the workplace, this is termed "burnout" and "low employee engagement."

I had a large group of managers from a multinational consumer goods company in a hotel conference room eager to learn more about culture and leadership effectiveness. I hung three posters that read I, WE, IT each positioned in different corners of the room. I described the three dimensions of success:

IT: Impersonal. Considers how to achieve the desired growth, profitability, and realization of mission or shared purpose of an organization.

WE: Interpersonal. Considers the relationships and trust between stakeholders. How do we collaborate and interact with one another to co-create our desired culture and community?

I: Personal. Considers the potential, sustainment of engagement, and need for meaning of each individual.

I asked them to reflect for a minute on which dimension they currently favored: *Where do you spend most of your time?* Then I invited them to get up and stand by the poster representing their answer. What do you think happened?

The majority moved to the IT, fewer moved to the WE, and less than a handful of individuals stood by the I. I asked them to consider the cost of focusing on that dimension at the expense of the others. Many revealed they felt burned out, uninspired, and reflected on which dimension needed more attention.

Three Dimensions of Success

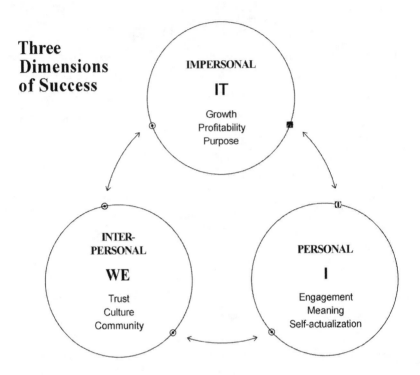

IMPERSONAL

IT

Growth
Profitability
Purpose

INTER-
PERSONAL

WE

Trust
Culture
Community

PERSONAL

I

Engagement
Meaning
Self-actualization

This exercise is a way to generate dialogue and increase awareness. These dimensions are interconnected and often hidden. The sustainability and viability of an individual and system depend on each dimension, even when we choose not to pay attention to them.

We have spent far too much energy emphasizing the impersonal at the expense of the interpersonal and personal dimensions. This approach contributes to our collective crisis of meaning, burnout, and a surprising number of people changing jobs to pursue something more satisfying. Poet William Butler Yeats writes, "It takes more courage to dig deep into the dark corners of one's soul and the back alleys of your society than it does for a soldier to fight on the battlefield." For the system to evolve, the individual participants must raise their quality of awareness and shift levels of consciousness.[3]

Success Beyond Success

When I opened the excommunication letter, I could not have articulated it then, but a part of me knew this process was not right. I know now and have the courage to say that others do not define who I am and decide my worth. A church is an institution created by humans, subject to bias, fallibility, and blind spots. And, like most human-made entities, churches decide to protect their interests and maintain power by exerting authority over others.

As more people determine how they want to direct their life, they will challenge institutional norms that don't make sense or seem right. More people are seeking to work for organizations that consider humanity's fate and that have a positive impact on the planet. In growing numbers, employees want to feel proud of the companies they work for.

There is a teaching in Conscious Business called "success beyond success." Success is getting the results I want in alignment with my vision and goals. "Success beyond success" is making choices and behaving in a way I feel proud of, consistent with my values and a sense of purpose.[4]

I do my best to honor all of the teachings shared with me on my journey that are universal truths and the pioneering spirit of my ancestors. I strive to see myself as both spirited and imperfect. I work to see my suffering as part of our shared humanity. This approach helps me feel empathy for others who are also suffering and to be a force for compassion.

A Better World

In the words of the graceful Audrey Hepburn, "Nothing is more important than empathy for another human being's suffering. Nothing. Not a career, not wealth, not intelligence, certainly not status. We have to feel for one another if we're going to survive with dignity."

The pandemic was a disorienting event for everyone. It invited us to reevaluate and regroup on a collective scale. It was like the universe said: "Okay. We're all going back to our homes now. We're coming back into ourselves to check in on our physical, mental, emotional, and spiritual well-being."

And then, a lot of harder stuff happened. We witnessed what had been going on for centuries come to the surface: severe racial injustice, political division, and serious mental health concerns. While we had more time to check in with ourselves, we also observed suffering up close. And it was everywhere.

Who do we need and want to be now?

Let's widen our lens. We have spent so much energy developing technologies to make life easier and more efficient, yet in many ways life feels harder. We desperately need to focus our attention on easing human suffering, increasing well-being for ourselves and others, and finding significance. Let's hold a larger vision of who we can be collectively and our potential for goodness.

Chapter 3

Significance

There is a wisdom in us that is more powerful than our despair.
Rolf Gates and Katrina Kenison[1]

Significance is knowing life's inherent value and using this wisdom to cultivate a life that matters. We unconsciously repeat thinking and behavior patterns throughout our lives. These patterns become part of us. They play out as our histories, impacting not only ourselves but our society and families. After my excommunication and my brother's death, I found my way back to two pieces of wisdom: that my value is inherent and that I am part of a whole. My perspective shifted, and I began to think about myself and life in new ways.

We move in two levels of existence: individual and collective. Finding significance happens in the space between these realms. What we see in others and what they see in us matters. We experience our wholeness in relationship to the whole. In times of despair and disillusionment, we can help one another to remember our potential, to feel we matter, to return to belonging.

The Idea

I hypothesize that there are three ways people infuse their experiences with meaning and find significance in life: Challenge, Work, and Love. Challenge is choosing courage during difficulty; Work is doing something to contribute; Love is caring for yourself, others, and our world.

I started interviewing people and recording their stories to explore my hypothesis. I asked them to describe the three most meaningful experiences that had shaped who they were or had influenced the trajectory of their life. I invited the same people to participate in a quantitative questionnaire to see if we could replicate the qualitative results.

How Do I Find Significance in Life?

The meaning interview is a compelling way to explore what experiences have the most meaning for you. Many of the interviewees asked if they could have a family member, friend, or colleague interview with me. I encouraged them to use the following script and experience it themselves.

The Meaning Interview Script

Set the context: I am going to ask you to share three of your most important life experiences, your feelings about each experience, and their meaning for you. I am going to listen without interrupting. When you are finished sharing your experience, I will check in with you to see if you are complete or if there is more you want to express. I will do this for each of the three experiences. Are you ready to begin?

Say: Tell me about an experience that shaped who you are or significantly influenced your life. What about this experience was most important or meaningful?

Ask: Do you feel complete? Do you have more you want to say?

Repeat for experiences two and three.

I invite you to try it. Use it with your clients, family, and friends. Below are lists of themes and language for each meaning indicator.

Meaning Indicators

These lists are a starting point for reflection on how you find significance in life.

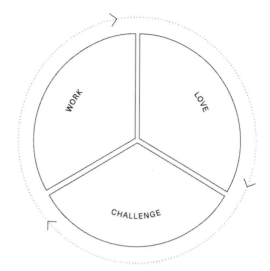

WORK:
DOING SOMETHING TO CONTRIBUTE

Progress
Serve
Calling
Cause
Responsibility
Ethics
Business
Build
Found
Mission
Create
Career

LOVE:
CARING FOR YOURSELF, OTHERS, AND OUR WORLD

Passion
Relationships
Joy
Beauty
Kindness
Nurture
Forgive
Encourage
Gratitude
Value
Connection

CHALLENGE:
CHOOSING COURAGE DURING DIFFICULTY

Personal power
Health
Loss
Death
Crisis
Overcome
Perseverance
Risk
Aspirations
Relocating
Grief
Resilience

Here are some of the stories shared with me during the interviews and their Meaning Indicators.

Challenge

In her last year of graduate school, Bonnie's younger brother was diagnosed with a rare kind of cancer called synovial sarcoma. He said to her, "I don't know what's going to happen, but I know that this will significantly change my life." He died eight months later.

The last conversation Bonnie had with her brother before he passed away was probably the most significant exchange she ever had in her life. It was a hard conversation. She asked him what he thought happened when you die. They both decided they didn't know and made the decision that they would see each other again in another life. Then Bonnie asked him, "What can I do for you?" Robert said, "If you had a gun, that would be the only thing you can do for me because I'm in so much pain, I don't want to do this anymore."

Bonnie's perception of things changed after Robert passed away. Things that she thought were important weren't quite so significant anymore. Before his death, she focused much of her energy on doing well in school. But what became meaningful afterward were her connections to people. She grew closer with her other brother. She held her mother in higher esteem knowing it took her all her strength to get out of bed every day and still go on living.

Challenge is choosing courage during difficulty. Bonnie's primary meaning indicator is Challenge. Some challenges cause us to consider our mortality or upend one's identity. When something unexpected happens that causes pain and suffering, most people experience a profound shift in perception. The illusion of separation and control fades. The death of a loved one is an example, like Bonnie losing her younger brother, but it could also happen through a chronic or acute health issue, a job loss, or a natural disaster. There are also challenges we embark upon due to aspiration or invitation.

It was 1998, and the World Cup was happening in France. Emily was a very introverted high school student living in Kenya. She had immersed herself in studying French, having discovered a love for the language. The French Embassy was putting on an international competition for high schoolers to show off their soccer knowledge. They invited representatives from different countries. Emily was invited to represent Kenya and her high school in the competition because of her French language skills. But Emily hated soccer.

During the trip, the group visited many cities in France. She experienced the culture and food while practicing her French. They even went to the ambassador's house. Emily's confidence and exposure began to grow. Because Emily didn't know much about soccer, she had to google basics like how many people were on a team and translate the answers to French. The high school competition was on TV. It was a big deal.

In the end, Emily won the competition. It was a moment of immense pride for her and her family. It showed her anything was possible, and that she didn't have to be an expert at everything. The French language opened opportunities for her, including new friendships. Emily learned she was capable and that she could do more through her gifts. She learned she could create opportunities for her family. "They don't teach you how to do that in school. Exposure is an equalizer," she said.

When speaking about challenges, the interviewees told stories about grieving the loss of loved ones, having near death experiences, and recovering from abuse and violence. Others talked about addressing mental health conditions, healing shame and trauma, and stopping cruelty and harm. Their stories also included themes of moving to another location or country, showing courage during a crisis, and persevering when they wanted to quit.

Whether the challenge is unexpected or chosen, it requires the individual and collective to gain more consciousness, strength, and energy.[2] Challenges are almost always an invitation to greater comprehension and can be catalysts for people to begin again from a different quality of awareness of who they are. They can be powerful moments for expansion and transformation.

Work

Randall grew up in a rural county in Kentucky. As a rising high school senior, he participated in the Governor's Scholars Program (GSP), a five-week summer residency program. Randall's academic focus that summer was math. The founder of Lotus Notes, Mitch Kapoor, was a guest speaker in one of Randall's small groups. It was 1984, and Lotus Notes had just launched a year earlier. It was exploding. Mitch made a big impression on Randall. Randall left GSP determined not to think small. His experience there was a great life lesson about saying yes to opportunity. He knew that opportunities as such were rare and that he should take advantage of them when they presented themselves.

Randall went on to found a software business, ArchVision, and then another company, AVAIL. He also co-founded a flexible workspace and business lounge called BaseHere, with multiple locations to serve Kentucky's entrepreneurs and creatives.

Randall finds significance in life when he is making, creating, or producing. For him, it's not about making money. It's about waking up every day to something that he's driven to do. He believes this increases happiness. This is what compelled him to found and scale multiple businesses straight out of college.

Randall's primary meaning indicator is Work. Work is doing something to contribute to society. Themes expressed where work was identified as the indicator of meaning included having stability, demonstrating responsibility, and career progression. Others talked about building a business or organization, creating something new, raising money, and pursuing ethics. Some discussed a call or dedication to a mission and contributing to a cause important to them.

Love

Sharon went to a Catholic, all-girls high school. There was a boys' Catholic school across the road. The bus ride home was the only time she saw teenage boys. She struggled to interact with them in a meaningful way.

One afternoon on the bus ride home, Sharon made a joke about one boy's physical appearance and said unkind things about him. The more her friends laughed, the more she got into it. Then she realized this boy was sitting not too far behind them. He'd heard everything that she'd said. She could see how embarrassed, hurt, and trapped he felt.

In this moment, she realized that what she had been saying was mindless and thoughtless. She didn't know this boy. She had never interacted with him. She was doing this to get the desired outcome, to get affirmation from her friends. Seeing his hurt, she thought about all of the ways she had been hurt before. Sharon made the intention never to do that again. Since that experience, Sharon has cared about how she conducts herself. She strives to be conscious and deliberate with her words and relationships.

Sharon's primary meaning indicator is Love. Love means caring for yourself, others, and our world. Many interviewees shared stories about working on relationships, caring for loved ones or raising children, and forgiveness. They expressed deep appreciation and gratitude, and spoke about the importance of friendship and connection. Others mentioned finding significance through healing, learning to love themselves, and experiencing beauty as well as protecting our physical world.

Interview Findings

The first round of Meaning Indicator interviews included 30 people. Interviewees participated from eight different countries with the majority living in the United States and identifying as White/Caucasian/European. Two-thirds identified as female and ages ranged from 30 to 80. Most participants had at least a Bachelor's degree and there was a lot of diversity in how participants identified their industry; most industry categories only had one participant.

Interviewees were asked to identify their three most important life experiences. To determine the indicator for each story shared, we generated a list of the language and themes expressed by category and calculated usage. When multiple themes were present from different categories, we used the language count to ultimately decide the meaning indicator. For instance, when the word "loss" showed up we counted it towards Challenge. When I explored these constructs from the total number of experiences shared, 57% of the experiences were categorized as Challenge, 24% were categorized as Love, and 19% were categorized as Work.

We identified a participant's primary indicator when two of their three experiences fall into one meaning indicator. Challenge was the primary indicator for 63% of the interviewees. Work was the primary indicator for 20% and Love was the primary indicator for 17%.

We determined a participant's secondary indicator based on one of their three experiences being coded as that meaning indicator. Love and Challenge were the secondary indicators for 33% of the interviewees. Work was the secondary indicator for 10%. Every participant did not have a secondary meaning indicator. Seven participants shared experiences where all three of their stories had the same meaning indicator. For example, all three of Randall's experiences were in the Work category. Only one participant had experiences that were categorized in all three of the indicators.

Overall, I was surprised that so many people found significance through Challenges, including myself. I wondered if we would discover the same thing using a different approach.

Interpretation

After completing the interviews and analyzing the qualitative data, we conducted a pilot study to see if we could convert this into a questionnaire-style quantitative instrument. Following months of waiting, I received the results from the quantitative pilot study and learned we were unsuccessful at replicating the qualitative results with the quantitative instrument. I felt disappointed.

The pilot participants received the meaning instrument twice. Once, when they were instructed to think about significant events in their lives before answering the scale, and again when we asked them to list three significant events in their lives before answering the scale. We divided the participants into two groups based on which of these versions they received first.

None of the participants in the pilot study selected the line items on either the thinking or listing format of the questionnaire that indicated Challenge as their primary meaning indicator. Only 16% chose the line items on the thinking format that indicated Challenge as their secondary meaning indicator, and only 20% chose the line items on the listing format that indicated Challenge as their secondary meaning indicator. The majority chose the line items that indicated Love as their primary meaning indicator on both the thinking and listing formats. In other words, when talking about their three most meaningful experiences the majority of people speak about Challenges but when rating items on a list they choose items for Love.

When I started the project, I hoped to create line items that people would rate for each indicator. Ideally, these would mimic the results of the interviews, and this would be a way to measure what matters easily. But we weren't even close.

Fortunately, I spoke with a friend and researcher who encouraged me to reconsider the efficacy of our qualitative research. I revisited the stories and their themes, looking for insights. I reflected on my thousands of conversations since I started coaching and what people talk about. I requested and read additional research papers on thematic analysis. I had conversations with friends and colleagues trying to make sense of why there was such a stark difference.

One conversation was particularly insightful. A friend shared a very traumatic experience she had in her early life. She indicated that this would be one of her three experiences if I were interviewing her. However, she wouldn't have chosen to check that on a questionnaire or even write it down as then it would become part of her identity. I wondered if this was true for others.

I continued to reflect on the themes of the interviews and how heartfelt the participants were in sharing their experiences. I felt honored to witness their soul's discoveries. Then I found my way back to the origin of the book and project when I was reading *Man's Search for Meaning*. I came across a page in my journal where I sketched out the initial idea with the meaning indicators and the following wisdom:

Infuse your experience with meaning that feels loving and empowering and opens a door for you to embrace life

Opening a Door to Embrace Life

The stories show us how we do this. They remind us there is collective wisdom we access as human beings. Wisdom is discovered and rediscovered within our consciousness. A list can't give us wisdom. In the next three chapters, I will share the ways we find our significance through Challenge, Work, and Love. *How we think, feel, and talk about things matters.*

Similar to many interviewees, my primary meaning indicator is Challenge. My secondary is Love. Many of my life experiences, including trauma and loss, grew my capacity for self-love and acceptance. I am learning to value myself and to feel I am worthy of love. I am learning to connect with others from my personal power instead of pain and unconscious patterns. I am learning that I can make a meaningful contribution to building a better world.

We can find significance. It is a choice. Awareness of our significance shapes our relationship with life and our energy to act. No matter what you are currently experiencing, it takes courage to open your heart and embrace life's inherent value. You matter. You are part of a whole that is continuously taking shape. In the final chapter, I will address the fourth and most important dimension of meaning—Belonging—but before that, I will share with you the three evolutionary paths to finding and cultivating significance in our lives: Challenge, Work, and Love.

Questions for Self-Study

As you identify your own meaning indicators, reflect on the following and how you develop and sustain a sense of mattering in your life:

What makes life worth living?

What makes me feel like my life matters?

Chapter 4

Challenge

Life is difficult. This is a great truth, one of the greatest truths. It is a great truth because once we truly see this truth, we transcend it. Once we truly know that life is difficult—once we truly understand and accept it—then life is no longer difficult. Because once it is accepted, the fact that life is difficult no longer matters.

M. Scott Peck

Choosing Courage during Difficulty

I ran my first and only marathon seven months after our son was born. This seemed like a good idea at the time. I look back now and think it was a little crazy. I would get up at 4:30, or 5:00 a.m. on Saturdays to feed him and then meet my friends for our long run.

This was my first experience in the power of training the mind. I used a book called *The Non-Runner's Marathon Trainer* (Whitsett, 1998). In addition to the physical training schedule, the book includes a mental training plan.

His research emphasizes internal versus external locus of control. Internal locus of control means focusing on what you can control in a situation. External locus of control focuses on what is out of your control, like the weather. One of the exercises was to write a mantra or affirmation for the race and memorize it. The author suggested reading it morning and night and reciting it during the runs. Mine read something like, "I am a marathon runner. I keep running no matter the conditions."

I can't remember the rest of the mantra, but I remember my experience. My brain and body didn't believe that affirmation yet. It didn't matter. I trained my mind and body to believe and create that circumstance by doing mental and physical training. I finished the marathon without stopping and felt a different kind of empowerment than I had experienced before.

If Challenge is your primary meaning indicator, you likely feel stimulated when evolving beyond perceived limits. You allow difficult experiences to open your awareness, activate your power, and cultivate wisdom. You value growth, learning, and exploration. You appreciate life's inherent value and see challenges as a learning experience and opportunity.

How to Find Significance through Challenge

There are two categories of Challenge. Some challenges happen to us through unexpected adversity, and there are challenges we take upon ourselves due to aspiration or invitation. The more demanding or disorienting the event, the greater the opportunity for growth and expansion. Extreme challenges push us to our limits or the edge of what we think we can endure.

Regardless of the type of challenge, here are ways to think about and respond to difficult circumstances that feel loving and empowering. You can advocate for change. You can choose to see the challenge as an opportunity for growth. You can choose to focus on the elements that are within your control. And you can practice acceptance, surrender, and letting go of resistance to what is happening.

The majority of the participants who shared their stories in the qualitative interviews had at least one story of challenge. There were stories of failure, divorce, illness, loss of a loved one, other losses, poverty, oppression, abandonment, abuse, betrayal, and other sufferings. Others shared stories of leaving their country of origin, quests for spiritual transformation, and participating in intense physical or intellectual competitions.

People who are looking for meaning often go to challenge and struggle. In a recent study linking meaning and health, the authors share predictors of meaningfulness and predictors of happiness. While experiences that bring happiness focus on satisfaction and things going well, experiences that bring meaning involve struggle, stress, and doing things for others. Meaningfulness is about experiencing the challenges in life *and the joys* and being able to integrate across different experiences.[1] To find significance, we learn to hold the tension between what makes us happy and what makes life feel meaningful.

Predictors of Meaningfulness

Predictors of Happiness

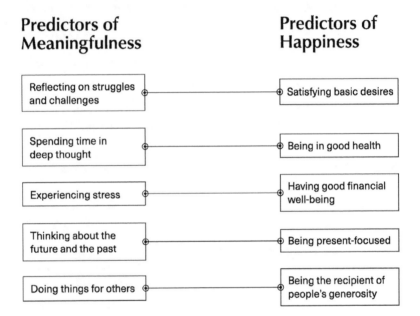

Predictors of Meaningfulness	Predictors of Happiness
Reflecting on struggles and challenges	Satisfying basic desires
Spending time in deep thought	Being in good health
Experiencing stress	Having good financial well-being
Thinking about the future and the past	Being present-focused
Doing things for others	Being the recipient of people's generosity

Challenge as Adversity

Adversity is misfortune, tragedy, or a difficult situation or condition. At its most extreme, people are required to fight for their lives. Some challenges are so traumatic that people don't overcome them. If you have experienced severe trauma, I recommend getting professional help to process it and begin healing. Therapy and counseling are necessary to address traumatic experiences adequately. It is a normal response to blame, shame, or feel guilt when terrible things happen. You might have questions like, *Why is this happening to me? What did*

I do to deserve this? What if anyone finds out? What will they think of me? Asking for help and getting support is the first act of courage.

When Diane was 29 years old, a guy broke into her house and attempted to assault her sexually. He held a knife to her throat. "What the fuck? Who are you? What is this?" she cried. Then out of nowhere, she let out a primal scream. Instinctively there was this power and inner strength to fight. She describes it as a sound she's never made or felt before, like an animal. This woke her roommate, who also started screaming. The attacker didn't know that there was someone else in the house. He ran out but left his knife with his fingerprints all over it.

After they caught him, the police brought him back to Michigan. Diane learned he had attacked over 40 women of all ages and broken into their homes before getting to her. It wasn't in the press, and the police weren't telling the story. The cops hadn't alerted the public because they didn't want to tip him off. When Diane discovered this, she became active with the story. She pushed the newspaper to write about it because people weren't aware.

Diane and a company she worked with printed thousands of copies of the article and left them in public places near the man's workplace. Diane's friends, who were attorneys, sprang into action. They helped create the now-universal law where victims have the right to speak when there is a plea bargain. Of the 40 women who could testify, most chose not to come forward. There were only three. Diane was one of them and felt very brave. Diane said, "This left me in my power."

Power is the will to act and generate strength. Like Diane, many interviewees shared how their challenges activated personal power they weren't aware of. They tapped into a part of themselves to survive and overcome.

Life Is Precious

Karen was driven by her need for security and safety. Because she didn't have children, she worried about earning enough money to take care of herself later in life. This drove her to hustle at work as an executive coach. And then she received a cancer diagnosis. Suddenly, she wasn't physically, mentally, or emotionally capable of hustling.

Facing her potential death brought her freedom. She realized that her previous drives weren't that important anymore. It took cancer for Karen to realize life is precious. Karen credits her self-development work as the scaffolding and foundation to get through cancer. She has a deeper level of compassion and recognizes that we never really know what somebody else is experiencing. That reminder has helped her not need to fix anything when working with her clients. She says, "When you have cancer, you don't know if it will be fixed or not. There's no right. There's no guarantee. You're at the mercy of the universe or God or whatever you want to call it. You can't control it."

What feels meaningful to Karen now is carving out time to do the things that bring her joy. This includes paying more attention to people. She goes at a slower pace. It is more deliberate. She is reclaiming spaciousness. She is finally living the type of life that makes her heart sing. So, "yay, cancer," as Karen says.

Facing your mortality or death of a loved one reminds us of two pieces of wisdom. Life is precious, and it is the small moments that make a life. How can we remember this in daily living?

Perspective Matters Most

In one of her most important studies, Stanford psychologist Laura Carstensen observed the emotional experiences of close to 200 people. She asked participants to carry a beeper 24 hours a day for one week every five years. During the week, they

---

Giving Thanks for Another Day

At the start of the day, wake up and touch your heart. Give thanks for another day of living and learning. Remember the impermanence of life and the preciousness of this moment. Pause and reflect upon your current reality, the challenges and opportunities this day holds. Then ask yourself:

What is most important for me to remember and keep in mind today?

Adapted from teachings of Joel and Michelle Levey

---

received random pages 35 times a day. Carstensen asked them to list all of the emotions they were experiencing at that moment. The study found that as people aged, they listed more positive emotions. Life became more satisfying. Her team concluded that living is a skill. Your needs and desires shift as you age from achieving, having, and getting to appreciating everyday pleasures and relationships.

Carstensen saw it differently. She proposed that it wasn't age but perspective. She had a near-death experience in her twenties that radically changed her viewpoint. While recovering, she thought very differently about what mattered to her. This informed her hypothesis, socioemotional selective theory, years later. How we spend our time may depend on how much time we think we have. When we see the future as finite and uncertain, our focus shifts to the here and now. We prioritize everyday pleasures and our closest relationships.[2]

In another study, her team examined how people spent thirty minutes of their time. The researchers found that regardless of age, when life begins to feel more fragile, people's goals and motives in their everyday lives shift entirely.[3] People worldwide have had a primer on life's fragility with the pandemic. I believe this fuels our collective crisis for meaning and the mass reshuffling in the workplace. It is perspective that matters most.[4]

See Your Challenge as an Opportunity for Learning

When things happen that you don't expect, it can seem like the end of the world. The essence of resilience is making conscious choices in the face of difficulty. You can expand your capacity for action by choosing your perspective and responding versus unconsciously reacting.

Connie is a human resource and administrative professional who lives and works in the Philippines. Early in her career, she focused on her work and would do anything to make her boss's life easier. She would even sleep at the office to finish everything demanded of her. Then Connie got into a car accident, and she began questioning what life was all about. She earned good money, but what was it all for?

She realized she felt burned out. Her life centered around her work. She was lonely. She decided to rest for a bit and let others take the lead. Then she had a falling out with her boss, and people started gossiping about her at work. She felt angry and hurt because of her predicament. Her good friends finally told her that she was being incredibly negative.

It took her several months to break out of this mindset. She did a lot of centering meditation. She recognized she was allowing others to decide for her and this relationship dynamic with her boss. She understood that she could choose how to respond and be proactive. She could bring her own weather by changing her life from the inside out. Connie had a choice. She decided her focus was no longer always prioritizing work. She decided to change her narrative and put meaning and purpose at her center. She refers to this as her learning agenda.

Connie's Learning Agenda

What am I good at?
What do I like to do for others?
What do I want to contribute?

Through reflection and meditation, Connie found a gift in the car accident. The accident helped her realize where she was putting her energy and where she wanted to put it. This was a significant shift in her perspective. She used this awareness to navigate her life with greater purpose and meaning.

We long to control the outcome in our jobs, personal relationships, and other pursuits. This makes it difficult to accept our circumstances when things don't turn out how we want. We might suffer from feelings of anger, blame, and resentment. One way to begin to move forward, similar to Connie, is to find the opportunity or learn in the experience.

If you cannot see a challenge as a lesson or gift yet, because it is too painful, you can work towards practicing acceptance. Acceptance is being with something without needing to change it. Surrendering is about trust. Trusting that you are worthy of love and this experience does not define your worth and who you are. It isn't easy, but working on a practice can help loosen resistance. Whether you call it surrendering, letting go, or releasing, it is ultimately about experiencing mental and emotional freedom in the face of extreme difficulties. This is one of the toughest practices. Here is a mantra I use as a reminder.

Mantra for Acceptance

I accept this for now and let it be.

The Paradox of Control

Constanza gave birth to her son, Agustin, by c-section in Mexico. He had apnea, and the doctors struggled to get him breathing properly. They put him in intensive care, and she went to a separate room to start recovering. Constanza was expecting the nurses to eventually bring her Joaquin, which was customary in Argentina, where she was from, but they weren't communicating with her, and she didn't know what was happening.

She eventually learned her son was in intensive care and needed a procedure. This was a dark moment. She was worried that Agustin might end up with a disability like her brother. He had also experienced a long birthing process and been deprived of oxygen. She worried that she wouldn't leave the hospital with him. After much mental anguish and worry, Constanza realized there was not much she could do. And she instantly felt calmer. She realized she had to surrender to trust and release her darkest thoughts. This experience helped Constanza recognize that some things were outside of her control. She could resist it, but that wouldn't solve it. Things soon turned around though. The procedure ended up working, and she was able to take Agustin home.

Focus on What You Can Control

Bring a challenge you are facing to mind. Reflect on the following:

What elements of the challenge are completely out of your control? (e.g., like the weather)

What are you most frustrated or anxious about?

What do you need to let go of to feel more at peace?

What 10% is within your control?

With this awareness, what do you choose to do?

Many of the Challenge stories I collected referenced this realization around control. This was one of the most powerful shifts in my perspective when I lost my brother. Realizing that some things are completely out of your control allows you to surrender the mental suffering and make sense of loss. However, when you perceive life as uncontrollable and unpredictable, it can also erode your sense of meaning. Distinguishing what you can control and what you can't is critical to coping with stress effectively.

Advocating for Change

Charla grew up poor in Chicago. As a young child, she lived in a tenement with her mother, father, and grandmother. They shared a one-room apartment with a public bathroom down the hall. When her grandmother went to apply for Social Security, she unexpectedly got a lump sum payment back. Charla's parents could now buy a two-flat building and rent one floor with those funds. Homeownership began to change their lives. Charla's family was eventually able to move, and out of the projects, transitioning from very poor to Black middle class, which was still very different from the white middle class in Chicago. There were still issues of safety; Charla knew which neighborhoods to avoid that were violent. It was a different kind of red-lining. "That sort of environment and our context of systemic racism doesn't allow for human beings to thrive," Charla shared.

Charla's grandmother worked as a maid. One of her clients paid for Charla's tuition to attend the University of Chicago's preschool and kindergarten. The rest of her education was at public schools and colleges until she went on to the University of Southern California for graduate school. Charla says that she didn't really experience white people until college because Chicago was such a segregated city. After graduate school, she lived in Germany for a while where she began to understand what living in close proximity to other cultures was like. Charla began to better understand her own history, as well as systemic problems. She saw what she and her family had overcome to succeed. Charla eventually became the superintendent of an affluent California school district at 35. She is now retired and volunteers as a political activist.

When Charla talks about her most important experiences in life, they involve people opening up the world for her, perseverance, and family. She credits the love and care of three adults as pivotal in creating her strong character and personality. She feels gratitude for education and opportunity. And she is grateful for the awareness she has gained about race and culture, about history and systemic problems. Her experience and knowledge are evident in her work and passions, such as universal preschool. She is passionate about the long-term effects of early education and has personally seen the difference it makes. She gets emotional when talking about it. Her early life experience in the projects fuels her activism and courage to fight for change for others.

The Better Side of Us

When Cynthia was ten years old, her parents bought a big, beautiful home in an upscale neighborhood. Before that, her nine-member family had lived in a three-bedroom, one-bathroom house. They were ecstatic and couldn't wait to have a big yard and their own rooms.

On the scheduled moving day, her parents left early to get everything ready, but due to an unfortunate event, they did not return until late that evening. They were the first African American family to move to this neighborhood, and hateful neighbors had vandalized their new home prior to their arrival. The neighbors had turned on the water hose and hung it from upstairs, ruining the wallpaper, carpeting, and more.

As kids, Cynthia and her siblings had no idea that this was a racist gesture. What she recalls most is her parents sitting the children down and explaining the situation. She still doesn't know how they did it, but her mother and father made her and her siblings feel safe and hopeful. Her parents assured them that they would clean up the house and were still moving. They communicated the plan so that Cynthia did not have any animosity for the people who did it. Cynthia says, "They modeled the better side of us."

By then, Cynthia was used to being the first African American at her Catholic school, at her church, and in other activities. But looking back, she realizes what a heavy burden it was to always be the first. She felt the high expectations, her parents always pressing them to be well-behaved. As Cynthia grew up, she resented that she had to live beneath this pressure, and as a result, she soon began to embrace the call to advocate for equity and anti-racism and tolerance in a multicultural world. She brought her personal experiences to her work as an administrator in a very integrated school system, and helped students come together racially and culturally.

These very different stories illustrate the roles race and discrimination play in lived experiences. For many individuals, Challenge is tied directly to perseverance in the face of racism and other injustices. Being a part of dismantling systemic inequities is what brings many individuals meaning. System-level challenges are an opportunity to disrupt our collective narratives and transform consciousness.[5] This creates the foundation for new thinking and systems that can benefit all of us.

Challenge as Aspiration or Invitation

Having aspirations can signal awareness of personal power or a position of advantage. Compared to complex social problems, we could judge individual aspirations as insignificant. This is false. It takes courage for anyone to aspire, dream, and take risks not knowing if they will succeed or not.

JJ started a swimwear business on the side while she was still working at her corporate job. The first couple of years were brutal, but she stuck with it. She faced many failures along the way and many times considered giving up. Her family and friends questioned why she was still chasing her dream as she worked long hours and learned to run a business, but JJ continued on, with little evidence that her dream of financial success and entrepreneurship would happen.

Against all odds, the business ultimately began making $25,000 a month in online sales. JJ describes how powerful it was to hold a vision and continue to see it through, even when it seemed more logical not to go forward. When things were difficult, JJ kept the faith; she did not allow herself to entertain the possibility of failure. Instead, she held her vision and committed to creating a business that aligned with her authentic self.

Following are some additional practices to explore if you chose Challenge as your primary Meaning Indicator. These are based on my experience and application in my own life.

Building Your Dream Muscles

If you have experienced difficulties or trauma in life, you might find dreaming or visualizing to be challenging. This was true for me. When you are just trying to survive day to day, it can be hard to imagine a different future might be possible. This also can be a way of protecting yourself from more pain and disappointment.

Here is a practice I have used over the past ten years to help build my dream muscles and consider what brings me joy, satisfaction, and fulfillment. I am still learning to create from my power instead of my pain. I harvest themes regarding my desires, choices, and preferences. It is a process of self-discovery. I challenge you to try it consistently for two weeks to see what surfaces.

Journal Questions

What do I appreciate?
How do I desire to feel?
What do I choose to do?
What do I ask life to provide for me today?

The Middle Way

The Middle Way is a process in Buddhism that involves direct investigation as we navigate life. At its core, it reminds us that life ultimately resists definition. As much as we crave certainty, new insights will always challenge our current beliefs and ideas. So, we must remain flexible and in "the middle." Personally, I spent so much time and energy during difficult moments wanting to capture the truth that I never arrived anywhere. I have learned that when it comes to knowing. I don't know what today will bring, and the world keeps changing.

Life is a work in progress, and the Middle Way can help us understand our relationship to life. Because we are interdependent, everything we do influences life. This reminds us that everything matters and protects us from meaninglessness. The Middle Way describes the open mind free of clinging to views. I can be unknowing and still respond clearly and compassionately to life's surprises. I can integrate the full range of my experiences, combining both my sorrows and my joys.

In coaching, we learn about polarities. They are pairs of opposites that are both strengths or values needed over time for a healthy, thriving self, or organizational system. For example, sorrow and joy. Both are necessary for a fulfilling and meaningful life. The Middle Way reminds us to look for the interdependencies and not overvalue one of the poles.

Comprehension Styles for Challenge

Comprehension styles are narratives that help us make sense of who we are and our experiences. They are the lens through which we tell our story. Challenges are an invitation to have a greater comprehension of our personal power. Whether the challenge is unexpected or chosen, it requires us to increase strength, energy, or consciousness. If we choose to see challenges as an opportunity for growth, they can inspire deeper thinking and to reflect on what matters. They can be powerful moments for expansion and transformation. Through Challenge, we deepen our self-trust as we explore the meaningfulness of new experiences and emerge with new perspectives:

- Practicing acceptance of life's difficulties *and* remembering your personal power
- Focusing on what is in your control *and* letting go of what is out of your control
- Seeing challenges as an opportunity for growth *and* releasing blame and shame
- Advocating or fighting for change *and* showing the better side of humanity

Find What Is Indestructible

Sometimes the only thing you can do is survive certain experiences. You wish you were thriving, but deep down, you feel worn out, you feel broken, you feel weary, you feel lost, you feel forsaken, you feel desperate, you feel grief, you feel afraid, you feel angry at life.

Surviving and thriving is a dance between polarities. Expecting that one condition is superior sets you up for disappointment and unrealistic expectations. Nature isn't always thriving. Living things die. Honor surviving and finding what is indestructible in you.

Expansion, growth, and transformation are happening during difficulty. Parts of us die off and make room for other parts of us to emerge. That said, we typically don't integrate and feel whole again until we reflect, look back, and make meaning out of our experiences. Knowing this reminds us to choose courage during difficulty and be compassionate with ourselves in the unknowing. The whole of life is a beautiful mystery.

Chapter 5

Work

Your work is to discover your work and then, with all your heart, give yourself to it.

Buddha

Doing Something to Contribute

The average person will spend over 90,000 hours at work during their lifetime. This is one-third of your life.[1] Another third will be spent sleeping which leaves a third for everything else. If Work is your primary meaning indicator, you probably feel most happy and fulfilled when engaged in stimulating tasks. You value progress and seeing your efforts produce a desired outcome. This helps you feel like you matter and that your life makes a difference.

I am fully aware and sensitive to the reality that many of us are lucky to do work we love and get paid for it. Others do not have work opportunities that feel fulfilling. I also appreciate those who came before us, our ancestors, upon whose shoulders we stand. Many previous generations worked tirelessly to create opportunities for future generations. Many BIPOC (Black, Indigenous, and People of Color), immigrants, and women didn't have the freedom to do the work they wanted. Structural racism, sexism, and unequal laws grew unequal institutions, oppressing these groups.

Even if Work is not your primary meaning indicator, it is important to learn to find significance in what you do because you will spend so much time working. Work, life, organizations, and society are so interconnected that finding meaning at work contributes to fostering meaning in your life.

How to Find Significance through Work

We think about work in several different ways. Sometimes, work is just a job, a means to a paycheck. It might be an important step on a career path leading to a desired role or opportunity. For some, work is a calling or a vehicle for deeper personal meaning and purpose. Work can also be in service of progress, to bring forward something for the greater good. Here are stories that show us how we can infuse our work with greater significance.

Work as Just a Job

Early in my coaching career, I was on a team with a project lead named Tom. One of our colleagues was struggling with the team dynamics, and her attitude was beginning to impact the rest of us negatively. Tom reminded her that there would be ebbs and flows in how we feel about our work, and he communicated that her behaviors were beginning to sabotage our collective efforts. She shared that she felt burnt out and probably needed to make a change, but the timing wasn't right yet.

In one of our team meetings, Tom asked what was most important to her. She spoke about her two teenagers and how she wanted to help them go to college. For her, the work was just a job, yet she could connect to why her job was important. It was her family. She put up a picture of her two children in her office. Each time she felt frustrated, she would look at that picture and remind herself of why she was there.

There will be periods of our life when our work no longer feels fulfilling or of importance. In these moments, we probably refer to work as just a job. This practice helps access a different feeling about a task or job by connecting it to a larger sense of importance.

To infuse your experience with more significance and find what feels motivating, ask yourself:

Why am I doing this?

Consider your current job. Where are you struggling for motivation and focus?

Describe why you are in that job.

Then identify which reasons feel like shoulds and which reasons feel mobilizing and inspiring.

When we are able to link our actions with a strong why, it inspires and motivates us to keep going even in the face of difficulty.

For my colleague, connecting with her genuine desire to provide for her children's college education created more joy in her work responsibilities. It allowed her to contribute to a better future for her children. She felt proud of this accomplishment and what she was achieving on their behalf. She was able to let go of feelings of obligation and frustration and feel more fulfillment. She could see she was making a difference for her family.

People also do their jobs to financially support themselves and their families, to pay for school or travel, and to learn something new or gain experience.

Work as an Important Step in a Career Path

Sometimes work can serve as an education in skills. When Nick went to work at a local Juicery, he described himself as a "dreamer with a bunch of ambitions and a bunch of ideals." What he lacked were the management skills to bring his ideas to fruition.

In his role at the Juicery, he learned how to become more structured and take action. He couldn't wait around for someone else to tell him what to do. In this fast-paced environment, he had to take initiative as a leader and learn how to work with different types of people. While he sometimes stumbled, Nick ultimately learned lessons to take him through life. He experienced some of his limitations, including wrestling with his ego when given power. He describes it as getting a crash course in entrepreneurship, business management, and personal growth.

Nick knew he was gaining skills and building capabilities to help him with his business ventures and career opportunities. When you choose to view your work as a development for a future goal or pursuit, you can feel greater fulfillment in the process. Reflection is a great tool to solidify your learnings and use them to create new possibilities.

Looking Back and Looking Forward

Looking back:

How did I grow or change because of this experience?

What did I learn about myself that I didn't know before?

What am I proud of or appreciate?

Looking forward:

What skills, abilities, or new ways of thinking have I gained through this experience that will help me in the future?

What is possible for me now?

Work in the Context of Meaning and Purpose

Two years out of law school, Lisa received an opportunity to practice in a private law firm specializing in business litigation. Previously, she had served as an assistant district attorney. All of the partners at the firm were relatively young with families. And there was one woman who was a partner. This was encouraging to Lisa.

However, within a year of Lisa joining the firm, the female partner left. Lisa quickly learned that the referral of new business was a significant marker of success. The firm developed business by building relationships with key referral sources.

The male partners took these men out to network and socialize for weekends, often including a trip to a strip club. As the only woman in the firm, Lisa was directed to entertain the men's wives with an evening of musical theater. Because of this arrangement, referrals seldom came to Lisa.

While Lisa was a skilled attorney, she had an epiphany that this was not the place for her. This was the mid-1990s, and although she knew she was the victim of sexual discrimination, she chose not to complain. And she didn't have another woman to talk to about it.

This experience prompted Lisa to reevaluate her career and purpose. One of her dreams was to work in a foundation and use her law degree for good—to work in a charitable or civic context. Lisa took the time to conduct a thoughtful job search to find the right fit. She ultimately landed in a leadership role at a foundation.

Lisa's time at the law firm helped her realize how she wanted to use her skills and use her time. She says that that particular time in her life helped her reorient; it inspired her to pursue her true passions. For the last 23 years, she has spent her career in philanthropy creating more just, vibrant, generous, and giving communities.

When we perform work in the context of a higher meaning and purpose, we connect our work to something of personal importance and the greater good. We think about it in the context of who we are being in the work, what we value, and how our contribution matters. You can use this exercise to explore what is meaningful and purposeful to you in your current work.

What Is Meaningful and Purposeful for You?

Close your eyes and imagine the end of your life. You are looking back at the work you are doing today.

What aspect would still seem meaningful?

What way of looking at it could make it even more meaningful?

What would make you feel glad you did this work?

Perhaps it is the difference you are making or the relationships you are building. Maybe it is the opportunity to mentor and develop other people. It could be the satisfaction of innovating or being part of a dynamic team.

Now think about your work and what you want to do well.

How will you approach your work this week?

What do you want to worry less about?

A lot of resistance to change comes from worrying about making a mistake or failure. This blocks creativity, innovation, and joy. When I first started my business, I found many of the tasks highly stressful. I was doing a lot of things I didn't know how to do yet. I would find myself questioning my capability as I was learning new things. This is common.

However, when I would connect back to how I wanted to approach my work, I came back to who I wanted to be while doing the work. I want to be open and curious to opportunities, willing to take risks, compassionate with myself and others, and playful. I was able to focus more on the process than the outcomes. I began to find more ease and was able to be of greater service. I felt more relaxed and confident.

It is unrealistic to find your work consistently meaningful. You are not your job. Your work is one vehicle for finding significance. There will be meaningful moments. Reflection exercises, such as the questions above,[2] can increase connection to what you find purposeful and meaningful now. When you align with this clarity, synchronicities and new paths often emerge.

Work as Progress

Patricia lives in Brazil. She describes her sabbatical year as saying yes to a call. She visited different eco villages, learning centers, and intentional communities in 11 different countries.

She had been part of a community called Pioneers of Change that met annually for many years, but when Patricia's father passed away, she felt a new sense of urgency to do work that mattered, and her day job offered her a sabbatical to pursue her mission. The principles guiding Patricia were, "Be yourself. Do what matters. Start now. Never stop asking questions. Engage with the community."

Patricia flew from the south of Brazil to England to launch the project. She talked with over 200 people and created the methodology for her research about learning communities. During that trip, she felt completely aligned and in flow, living many synchronicities. She came across amazing people and experienced a different level of openness in her mind and heart throughout this process. The work she started then continues to grow and thrive now, bringing together changemakers from all walks of life.

Progress is growth or movement to a better condition or higher state. When people use their work to do something in service of the collective well-being, they create meaningful transformation for themselves and others.

Comprehension Styles for Work

Many believe that it is necessary to sell out in order to achieve economic success or drop out to pursue a meaningful life. This is a false polarity. When business is conducted as an

expression of your core values there is harmony between material and spiritual wealth.
Fred Kofman

Comprehension styles are narratives that help us to make sense of our experiences and who we are. In the context of Work, here are some of the tensions in business when considering the greater good, meaning, and happiness:

- Interdependence/part of a whole *and* independence
- Sustainability *and* growth/expansion
- Profit *and* people

You need these tensions. Both are valuable. But without awareness of these tensions, businesses would not be able to forge ahead as a force for good.

Culture at Work for the Greater Good

As part of my work as a Culture Consultant, I work with culture archetypes based on the work of Carolyn Taylor, founder of Walking the Talk. When she first wrote her book, she identified five organizational archetypes: Customer Centric, One Team, Innovation, Achievement, and People First.[3] Each archetype has specific characteristics, including the underlying beliefs and values and the behaviors, systems, and symbols that define the workplace culture.

In the last decade, a new archetype has emerged called the Greater Good. The defining attribute of this culture is that people are expected to contribute to the well-being of the larger community. The organization considers that they have a responsibility bigger than simply meeting the needs of their customers. They are looking at their impact on the community and the world as a whole. They care about social responsibility, the environment, meaning, sustainability, and making a difference.

One of the challenges of Greater Good organizations is learning how to manage competing stakeholder needs. They are resolving paradoxes as they figure out how to fulfill their aspiration and deliver profit, how to manage short-term and long-term goals, and stay committed to their principles. They continually face the false dichotomy of making money or doing good.

B Lab, the nonprofit behind B Corps, describes it this way:

"Certified B Corporations are businesses that meet the highest standards of verified social and environmental performance, public transparency, and legal accountability to balance profit and purpose. B Corps are accelerating a global culture shift to redefine success in business and build a more inclusive and sustainable economy."[4]

All B Corps undergo a rigorous certification process in several categories including governance, workers, community, and environment to assess their performance. Part of the free assessment measures a company's strengths and recommends areas for improvement. On the B Corp directory, you can view the score of any B Corp.

A B Corp where I helped conduct a culture diagnostic had committed to reducing their impact on the environment and being stewards of positive impact for their community. Ninety-five percent of what you buy in their shops is reusable, recyclable, or compostable. As they work towards zero waste in their shops, they have diverted more than 100 tons of waste from landfills.

In 2015, they faced a challenge that tested their commitment to these principles. They found a product with listeria in it. The leadership team met to discuss what to do. Ultimately, they decided to recall $2 million worth of product. This was a massive recall and required closing stores for a week. They chose to stand by their commitment to be stewards of positive impact on their community and walk their talk in service of the greater good.

One of the employees described how impactful it was to be present during those tough decisions. It confirmed his belief in the leaders of the company and their commitment to who they are as a company. This was a huge shift for the business, and it took until 2020 to recover fully.

Losing sight of its vision is a deal killer for any organization. I find it encouraging that this organizational archetype is growing and we are seeing more socially conscious aspirations where profit and purpose are learning to thrive together.

Meaning of Work

Group norms are the guiding behaviors of a team. They are embedded in an organization's culture and team subcultures. In 2012, Google launched Project Aristotle to understand why some teams were more effective and successful than others. They gathered data, assessing 180 Google teams over four years. At first, the metrics did not provide clear insight. But after looking more closely, they realized that group norms were the key to teams' success. The final learnings concluded that who was on the team mattered less than how the team members interacted, structured their work, and viewed their contributions.[5]

Google identified the following five specific group norms as the keys to success:

Psychological safety: Team members feel safe to take risks and be vulnerable in front of one another

Dependability: Team members get things done on time and meet a high bar for excellence

Structure and clarity: Team members have clear plans and goals

> Meaning of work: Work is personally important to team members
>
> Impact of work: Team members think their work matters and creates change

The fourth norm is meaning of work and the fifth norm is impact of work. For groups to be at their best, they need each person to connect to why their work is important to them. They also need to believe their work matters and creates meaningful change to sustain engagement.

Pursuing New Challenges

When you lose connection to why your work is important to you, you are less curious and less engaged in learning. Your work assignments cannot rely solely on your expertise and ability. Ideally, work also needs to match your growing interests and skills. This is why many organizations offer stretch assignments so people can pursue new challenges and expand their skill sets.

Feeling challenged can also contribute to profound moments of meaningfulness. One of the multinational technology organizations I worked with would rotate employees into new learning opportunities every two to three years as part of their development. If you are looking for growth opportunities and feeling stuck, consider asking if a stretch assignment is possible or if you can take a class you are interested in. There are many free, quality, online courses available through universities such as MIT and their Presencing Institute or companies such as LinkedIn. Another option is to find a mentor or coach to support you in exploring a change.

Mike, cofounder of ACT Leadership, describes his experience exploring a career pivot. He was miserable and burnt out with his first career as a CPA and consultant. Mike took on some pro-bono coaching and began to explore questions like: *What am I good at? What do I enjoy doing? What brings me joy?* He wishes he would have had these types of conversations when he was 18. Like many of us, he followed the more socially acceptable path of choosing a reputable, professional career. But he ended up hating it.

Twenty years later, Mike decided to get certified in leadership coaching and founded a coach training business with his wife, Erin. Initially, it was very tough financially, with very little income for the first two years. Mike had to have some tough conversations with his inner critic, who was questioning, doubting, and judging his decisions and ability. With the help of a coach, he was able to stay connected to his purpose and inner drive. The turning point was when they won their first substantial government contract to provide coach training for leaders. Weeks later they welcomed the arrival of their first daughter.

Mike feels privileged. He has worked hard. And he's had some luck along the way. But he also had opportunities that others don't always have. He is aware that a lot of people have a tougher time. His dad always reminds him to not get tempted to sit on what you have and become ignorant. In other words, don't become complacent and ungrateful. His work now is about service and being of service to others and doing it in a smart way.

A Meaningful Self at Work

Because we spend so much energy and time at work, what we experience at work shapes what we experience in life. There are different approaches out there to help organizations support their people in their search for meaning and connection. Coaching in the workplace is one way to help people look more deeply at the impact on their social relationships (WE dimension) and foster new self-awareness (I dimension).

We can self-actualize through work. In an Everyone Culture, Keegan and Lahey suggest work can be the catalyst for self-development and actualization.[6] We can design the cultural norms and interactions to support this process. One of the values of smaller firms is that, because of their size, they are able to facilitate the emergence of a meaningful self in a more effective way. The employees can more easily identify their personal contribution to the company's success. Leaders who foster, encourage, and appreciate workers prompt a more meaningful self at work.[7]

Work is such a huge part of our lives. And most of us want meaningful work. It's time to find an authentic connection between our work and purpose.

Questions for Self-Study

How is your work connected to what is most important to you now?

What are you most proud of or want to celebrate about your contribution through your work?

What is the impact or relevance your work has for other individuals, groups, or the wider environment?[8]

Chapter 6

Love

An awake heart is like a sky that pours light.
Hafiz

Caring for Yourself, Other, and Our World

My first career was teaching elementary school. I wanted to create an environment that was loving and welcoming. I believed students would flourish in an accepting and inclusive atmosphere. When I received the Teacher of the Year award for my school after my second year of teaching, I was surprised. I didn't know this award even existed. While I didn't have the expertise and experience yet, I did bring enthusiasm, passion, and care for my students.

My students were from all over the world, and many did not yet speak English. Others faced extreme financial or cultural challenges in their lives and had no power to change these situations. I came home most days and cried. I could not change their circumstances outside school, but I wanted them to know and feel their worthiness and potential. I reminded myself that I could do my best to see and reflect their value. I knew this could have a ripple effect on what they believed about themselves, others, and our world.

If Love is your primary meaning indicator, you experience a sense of life's inherent value through relationships, joy, and beauty. You most likely feel aliveness and fulfillment when you are nurturing people, animals, or our planet. Nurturing is caring for others and encouraging them through words and actions. You feel things deeply, follow your passions, and value harmony.

How to Find Significance through Love

All of us want unconditional love. It is the capacity to choose the vulnerability of relationships and heartbreak despite seeing the worst aspects of humanity. Without vulnerability, there is no intimacy. One of my teachers says intimacy is *into-me-see*. It feels risky to let people see the parts of ourselves we want to keep hidden for fear of judgment or rejection. Sometimes these parts are even hidden from ourselves as they are too painful to face yet.

Spiritual teachings show us a roadmap of how to find significance through Love. Taoism teaches us about self-love and self-worth, Judaism and Christianity teach us to love our neighbors as ourselves, and Buddhism teaches us about loving-kindness and the path to enlightenment. They hold the wisdom that there is inherent value to life, and our value is inherent, too. They remind us we are spiritual beings having a human experience and that we are all interconnected.

In *Self-Delusion: The Surprising Science of How We Are Connected and Why That Matters*, Tom Oliver talks about how we are seeing a genuine synergy emerging between science and spirituality in the twenty-first century. It is called evidence-based spirituality. Researchers are exploring scientifically the moral and spiritual states that have typically been dubbed religious experiences and how our brain states change. He shares scientific studies related to the three dimensions of interconnectedness: interconnectedness to our inner ecosystem for a healthy body and mind, our connectedness with nature, our interconnectedness with other people.[1]

Regardless of wisdom, tradition, or science, these teachings show us how to be in a wise relationship with ourselves, others, and our world. A wise relationship means doing no harm, and practical love is about wise action. We can take a stand for love by responding to a slight or injustice as a call for love instead of choosing to take it personally and inflicting more harm. I'll share three ways to think about finding significance through love.

Love as Caring for Yourself

I started learning to care for myself over a decade ago when I hired my first coach. I began practicing yoga once a week. At first, my self-care was more about the basics of exercising, healthy eating, and taking time for myself. I learned how to ask for help and to set boundaries. Exploring and prioritizing my needs seemed radical at the time. I had spent so much of my life taking care of others that I didn't understand that I needed to learn to love and care for myself, too. I learned that making self-love a priority would help me love without resentment or martyrdom.

While I know this now, it has been difficult to practice empathy and self-love consistently. I am aware of how strong my inner critic—the judge—still is. I am learning to see beauty in my imperfections and the imperfections of others. To fully experience love from another, you must love and accept yourself fully.

One way to check how you treat yourself is to notice when you are being self-critical. In coaching, we call this voice the judge or inner critic. It might be that this voice is so familiar that you don't even pay attention to it. For example, when you fall short of your standards or fail, your judge might say something like, "you idiot," "why even bother or try."

Observing Your Inner Critic

What words do you use when you are being self-critical?

What is the tone of voice?

How do you react or feel when you say this to yourself?

Some coaches and their clients give their inner critic a name. One dear friend and colleague calls hers Brunhilda. When she shows up in our conversations, she will acknowledge her and say something funny like, "There's Brunhilda again." We will laugh and then she will come up with something more kind to say to herself instead.

Speaking Kindly to Yourself

The inner critic never goes away. When we get to know this part of ourselves, we can challenge the thoughts and lies of the inner critic when we observe them. For example, a common thought of the judge is, "If I don't make you feel bad when you fail at something or make a mistake, then you won't change."

In a study regarding attitudes toward guilty eaters, researchers asked a group of women to eat a donut within four minutes and then drink a glass of water to feel full. Some of the women received a message of self-compassion. They were encouraged not to be so hard on themselves for indulging. The other group didn't get this message. Next in the study, the two groups of women were presented with bowls of candy and asked to eat as much or as little of the candy as they desired.

Which group do you think ate more candy? The group that received the message of self-compassion and self-forgiveness only ate 28 grams of candy. The group who didn't get those messages ate 70 grams of candy. They have termed this the "what-the-hell" effect. They found out that speaking kindly to themselves allowed the women to turn off the guilt rather than giving them a license to eat more.[2]

As you begin to notice when you automatically shift into self-criticism and beat yourself up, observe the reactions and feelings this kind of talk generates. Typically feelings of shame, guilt, and loss of control come from your own lies. These thoughts keep you in self-defeating patterns and encourage you to give up. The trick is to learn to speak to yourself kindly and shift into a mindset of self-compassion instead of self-judgment.

Seeing Yourself with Kind Eyes

David owned a successful business with his brother until their relationship fell apart, and he chose to walk away. David also went through a painful romantic relationship where he felt suicidal at one point. He felt lonely and hopeless and was in a very negative mindset.

David decided to take a class at the University of Santa Monica in spiritual psychology to reevaluate what he wanted to do. He was able to reframe some of his beliefs and let go of others that weren't very supportive. This class also helped him to transform some of his long-held beliefs about himself. Now, when he experiences negativity, he has more tools to work with. He understands these feelings are not permanent. David feels more hopeful and says this change has had a lasting impact on how he sees himself. This class was one of his most significant life experiences.

Then Covid-19 hit. With his new perspective, he saw an opportunity to practice and strengthen his resilience, rediscover peace, and restore confidence. And most importantly, he feels more hopeful. David explores what brings him joy and prioritizes being part of communities doing meaningful work around the world.

Like David, you can practice seeing yourself through kind eyes and experiment with new beliefs about yourself and the nature of others and the world. I will talk more about how to do this in Chapter 7. When things are especially challenging, and your inner critic is raging, you can try self-compassion.

Self-Compassion

When you have compassion for yourself, you accept your humanness and imperfections. While you might make changes to feel better, you do make those changes out of love and care for yourself versus not being good enough. The more you open your heart and accept your shortcomings, the more you experience compassion—not just for yourself but also for other people.

Many of us treat others better than we treat ourselves. When others are in pain or having a difficult time, we offer them care and comfort. We don't just tell them to suck it up and go on. We acknowledge it is difficult and encourage them. We can do the same for ourselves.

Kristin Neff teaches there are three parts to practicing self-compassion: mindfulness, common humanity, and self-kindness. Mindfulness is observing what is occurring in the moment without judging it as good or bad. When we recognize other people have the same experiences as us, we remember our common humanity. Self-kindness is offering yourself words of compassion in the moment.

Self-Compassion Practice

Bring to mind a situation in your life that is difficult for you.

As you think about it, notice where you are feeling the stress in your body.

Say to yourself, "This is a moment of suffering" or "This is stress."

Then say to yourself, "Suffering is a part of life" or "Other people feel this way too."

Place your hand on your heart. Say something like, "May I be kind to myself" or "May I be strong."

Adapted from Greater Good Mindfulness Practices Kit

While we might seem separate, we are all connected. Common humanity reminds us that we are not alone or that different in our struggles and joys. Loving ourselves and loving another person are the same thing. Social-network theory shows how we can influence others we haven't even met. The theory proves that our behaviors can impact up to three people. Being aware of our indirect effect on others encourages us to cultivate a healthy inner ecosystem and have a more compassionate approach to how we interact with others.

Love as Caring for Others

When Laura was 17, she moved out. Her dad was an alcoholic, and she was angry with him for being absent from her life. The anger was so intense that she didn't see an end in sight. Laura couldn't imagine how he could be a part of her adult life, but she didn't want him out of her life either.

When her paternal grandmother died, her dad drove to Colorado, where her family lived, to start the funeral and grieving process. Laura flew out to Colorado, but a giant blizzard hit and the rest of her family couldn't travel. She was there alone with her dad for two or three days.

They drove to the place where his mom used to live, and he told Laura stories about the loss of his dad many years earlier. For the first time, Laura felt empathy for her dad and reached for his hand. That softness and tenderness melted him. Laura's dad burst into tears. He said, "I am sorry. I am such a failure." Moved by his sincere apology, Laura said, "I forgive you. I forgive you."

That was the turning point for Laura. She began softening her anger and resentment and even hate. While their relationship will never be what she wished she could have, she feels close to him. This wouldn't have happened without that blizzard. Laura says what was most significant about this experience was that she could either continue to hold her dad responsible for all of the things he ever did or forgive and release the anger and hate. She still feels her heart release when she talks about the gift of forgiveness.

Not all of us will have the opportunity to receive an apology from someone who has hurt us. We might still be carrying the pain and suffering. Forgiveness is not only for the person who has wronged us. Forgiveness is also for us to find freedom from reliving the harms inflicted in the past.

Integrity and Forgiveness

I have experienced many difficulties in my life. I have grieved deep loss and absorbed the sorrow of disillusionment. I have witnessed the worst of human nature and our ability to harm one another. I have wondered why people do such hurtful things to each other.

All the while, there was a parallel story happening. A story of joy amidst the suffering being inflicted. The same people who did terrible things were also generous, loving, and helping others. It is hard to make sense of it all and find our way to integrity and forgiveness.

Perhaps our greatest act of empathy is to accept people's complexities. To be with both their pain and their light and still find a way to love and forgive them. If not, we will harden and contract to life's grace and beauty.

I was introduced to a Hawaiian prayer called Ho'oponopono by one of my yoga teachers. It can help with your relationship with yourself, others, and the earth. It is a practice for forgiveness and reconciliation and making things right in your relationships.

It is an intention of holding space for repentance, forgiveness, gratitude, and transmutation. I have been using it by myself to release strong emotions and invite forgiveness of myself and others. I can feel the emotions release as I say the words in my head or aloud.

> **Forgiveness Practice: Ho'oponopono**
> Put your hand on your heart and imagine the person you want to forgive or to forgive you. Notice where you are holding any tension. Take a breath and invite yourself to soften. Imagine you are having a conversation with this person. It has four parts to it:
> I am sorry.
> I forgive you.
> Thank you.
> I love you.

When we forgive others, we are forgiven. When we focus on healing the past, we help heal life now. When we release feelings of anger and resentment, we can be present to the parallel story. We can choose appreciation for the experiences that shape who we become. It is easier to see others with kind eyes, act with compassion, and feel empathy.

Empathy

September 2021 marked 20 years since my brother, Matt, passed away. My mom, sister, Matt's widow, his daughter, and I got together on Zoom to share our memories of him. We laughed, we cried, and we mourned. After all these years, we still seek meaning from this experience, learning how it has shaped us differently.

I feel empathy for my mom in a way I couldn't all those years ago. I didn't have children then and hadn't experienced the depth of love you can feel for your child. Even imagining losing one of my children feels unfathomable today. It also felt too painful to be with her pain without being able to fix or solve it.

Consider your capacity to listen with empathy. Here is a spectrum shared with me by a colleague, Pablo Carter, adapted from the work of Stephen Covey.

Empathy: A Listening Spectrum

Level 1. I don't accept or join the other's feelings. We often do this with good intentions, e.g., to reassure. "Don't feel the way you do" messages.

A level 1 conversation might sound like this:

Dan: I am upset that Jack didn't thank me for taking him to his driving test.

Michelle: Well, what do you expect? He is only a teenage boy. I bet you didn't always thank your parents when you were a teenager. I know he appreciates you.

Level 2. I want to fix the problem (and make the feeling go away). We might feel with the other but, deep inside, we think we have "the obvious solution." We pass our message with sympathy, and, as with level 1, it comes from good intentions. When I listened to my mom many years ago, I was listening to her at levels 1 and 2.

A level 2 conversation sounds like this:

Denise: I am really angry that my boss took over my part of the presentation today.

Heather: I am so sorry she did that again. I think you should talk to her about how her behavior is affecting you.

Level 3. I ask questions and listen carefully. We refrain from imposing—or even suggesting—our way to solve another's problem. We are receptive. We listen in respectful silence. We ask relevant questions (inquiry) and explore what is the matter.

A level 3 conversation sounds like this:

Juan: I am tired of my employees making excuses for not getting their work done on time.

Scott: What's important about this focus for you today?

Juan: I got called out in a meeting for having three of our projects delayed. I am worried I might get demoted if I don't turn this around.

Scott: You seem really concerned. What would be an ideal outcome for our conversation?

Juan: I want to figure out how to have a productive conversation with the team leads about missed deadlines.

Level 4. I can acknowledge the emotion underneath the story fully. We feel what the other is feeling and can synchronize our emotional states effectively. Our inquiry and active listening focus on the emotional component of the story. Emotions are not deniable.

A level 4 conversation sounds like this:

Linda: I don't care if I get the promotion at this point. I have exceeded expectations for the past two years, and they still didn't offer me director. I don't know what else I can do.

Bart: I sense you might be disappointed and discouraged, maybe even a bit angry. How are you feeling?

Linda: Yes, I am pissed off and not feeling motivated.

Level 5. I am able to accompany the other in a deeper meaning. We can feel with another person and let them know it. We know how these emotions arise and how to honor them based on that knowledge. We feel with them but also understand the full impact of their emotions.

A level 5 conversation sounds like this:

April: I am so excited about being on the news and having the chance to share our story. I think it might help a lot of people.

Elan: I can feel your excitement and your eyes light up when you talk about it.

April: I also feel a bit nervous and unsure about what I will say. I am still struggling with losing Brian and being a single mom. I am still questioning why he had to die at such a young age. There are so many ups and downs, and I don't want to cry on the news. People have been really generous, and I want them to know their contributions made a difference.

Elan: It sounds like you are experiencing a lot of different emotions. I can hear the sadness in your voice now as you talk about Brian. What do you want it to feel like when you are sharing your story?

All these steps are incremental. There is no way to get to the next level without mastering the previous one.

At level 5, the listener accompanies the other person in deeper meaning. You can be with them in a range of emotions and hold space for this expansion. You remember the person is not their story or their emotions. You can experience the other person in their true nature and see them with kind eyes while they expose the full range of their humanity.

I want to say just a few words about practical love and the power of care with honesty. Sometimes self-concern and wanting to be liked can get in the way of expressing difficult truths in relationships, leading to ruinous empathy.[3] There is a saying I learned when giving tough feedback: kind eyes, sharp sword. Kind eyes are the empathy and compassion we hold in our hearts for the other person. Sharp sword is going in with clean energy and not mincing your words. It is directly sharing the impact the person's behavior has on you and others while owning any assumptions. One of my colleagues calls this type of conversation a care-frontation. What is distinct about a care-frontation versus judgment is that the other person trusts your intention? They believe you want the best for them.

Seeing Others with Kind Eyes

The inner critic or judge isn't only harmful to ourselves; it can be extremely harmful to others. It is easy to fall into the habit of looking for what needs to be better or fixed. This is also where most people have learned to listen (at a Level 2—see above example). So much of our work life in the Information Age is about continuous improvement, creating efficiencies, and solving problems, not about truly seeing or listening.

We aren't machines or technology, though. People are not problems to be solved or fixed, and we can't fix many of their problems because they involve other people. Working with human beings is about holding the tension of fear and love present in all of us with humility and curiosity.

In coaching, we are trained to look for and acknowledge the admirable characteristics we see in someone. For example, "You are persistent and courageous. People typically light up when they hear the good qualities you are seeing in them." Try this with your spouse, family, or a team you lead at work.

Appreciation

Ask each person to think of something they genuinely appreciate about the other person as well as the characteristics they see in them.

One person goes first and expresses appreciation for the person to their right.

The person receiving it only says, "Thank you." and then offers appreciation to the next person to their right.

If you have a small group of people, you could choose to offer each person appreciation.

When I do this with my husband, Dan, I remember how easy it is to take him for granted in daily life. I remember why I chose him as my partner, and I feel more loving. When we do this as a family, Addison's and Jack's eyes shine brightly; they smile and relax. They feel seen, and they show us they see us too. When I do this with teams, people often share things they have never acknowledged before about their colleagues.

Here are a few of the questions I use when doing this with teams:

- What successes do you want to celebrate since our last session?
- What do you most appreciate about members of your team?

While working with a financial services company on becoming a high-performing team, I kicked off their third offsite workshop with this practice. I took them through a brief mindfulness exercise focused on gratitude and then invited them to do a round of checking in using the above questions. As each team member shared what was going well and what they valued about their fellow teammates, the energy in the room shifted, and everyone could feel it. Appreciation is one of the highest states of energy and inspires creativity and receptivity. This set the stage for a dynamic day of collaboration and generating new awareness.

Whether you are strengthening your capacity to care for others or learning self-love and how to value yourself, the thoughts and behaviors are transferable. Forgiveness, empathy, and appreciation are ways of relating that move you beyond the ego. Transcending self-interest and serving others is an intrinsic human need and essential for having a life that feels meaningful and worthwhile.[4]

Love and Passion

Passion is what gives sense to our life.
His Holiness, the Dalai Lama

We are cartographers, and passion is how we create our life's map. We were each designed with seeds of desire, and as those seeds manifest in the physical form, we create our path in the world.

Listen to yourself and untangle yourself from the noise of others to find and follow your passion. You can't manufacture or force passion. You have to trust the longings of your heart and follow them like breadcrumbs as the path reveals itself.

Trusting the Longings of Your Heart

John is a musician and a drummer. He spent much of his time performing while in distress. When he played well, he was desperate for somebody to tell him they thought it was good, so he'd say to the other musicians, "Hey, you sounded great!" waiting for the return compliment. This was a very painful and angst-ridden process for John. His need to be recognized as brilliant ultimately caused him to push himself to overplay, to not listen to others, and not to feel connected. When he experienced failure, he would take that as confirmation of his unworthiness.

The roots of John's low self-worth began at an early age. John's father had repeatedly told him as a child that he was not good enough, and this practice caused John to develop a negative internal narrative. It also pushed him to believe that he must "be extraordinary or die." On top of this, John found that his mother gave him more attention when he was suffering, so he began to equate suffering with love and worth. As John moved through his 20s, he fell into a dark hole of despair. He also found himself attracted to women who were suffering, as both he and his mother were. John thought that if he could solve their suffering, he might feel valued and loved. It took time, but John eventually saw his suffering for what it was and where it came from. He knew he needed to work on building his self-worth.

John's life took on a different shape as he gravitated toward the drum circle world. He met a foremost trainer and facilitator.

John traveled with him and found it was fun, and he saw how other people were benefiting from these experiences. Soon, John's focus changed. He began to feel a deep sense of purpose from helping others and connecting them to their value so that they could be in full expression. This was an important shift for John, directly connected to meaning. Before, he was attached to being a known performer. But it became an act of self-healing, to not only be of service but to be in service. He describes it as healing the healer. When he leads a drum circle, he is part of a community. He feels connected and helps others feel the same.

Comprehension Styles for Love

Comprehension styles are narratives that help us make sense of ourselves and our experiences. When we follow the longings of our heart and allow our focus to expand beyond our fears and insecurities, we can move with greater trust and ease. Allowing is about trusting the process of life itself, exploring passions, and enjoying the mystery of the unfolding. Along the way, there are things you will not understand, and there are many questions that will remain unanswered, but having the courage to acknowledge the uncertainty and stay curious about sharing love is the connective tissue of your relationship with life itself. This practice will allow you to receive love and give your love without reservation.

Tensions to be with when caring for ourselves, others, and our world include:

- Integrity *and* forgiveness
- Giving *and* receiving freely
- Authentic expression *and* belonging
- Science *and* spirituality

Love as Caring for Our World

Caring for our world can include serving your family, friends, colleagues, strangers, animals, community, or society. It could also be taking care of the earth and focusing on environmental issues through protection, sustainability, and restoration.

In the interviews coded as Love, the participants shared stories about learning to love themselves and the relationships that had significantly impacted their lives. These relationships helped them think differently about themselves and others, and, in some cases, they also expanded their worldview. One interviewee, MJ, attended a leadership camp at age 17, that exposed her to different beliefs and Native American teachings. MJ had been raised Catholic, but at the camp she met people from various backgrounds with different beliefs, including her camp leader who was Jewish. She described her new experience as the start of her spiritual life. She began to see the world through the eyes of others.

These are stories of expansion and transcendence. They remind us that we are interconnected, and that love is what transforms our world. Love is a force within and around us. When we nurture and care for what we value, this is our love in action.

Questions for Self-Study

How is the quality of your relationship with yourself?

Which relationships could use greater empathy, forgiveness or appreciation?

What seems like the next stage of learning and growth for your relationships?

Chapter 7

Belonging

True belonging is an experience of connection to everything, and a sense of being a necessary part of the whole. When you belong, you know you matter.

Leza Danly[1]

The Great Pause

People are seeing life differently and reconsidering what matters. When the pandemic first hit, a friend invited me to a monthly coaches' group. We named our virtual gatherings the Great Pause.

We spent our time together talking about what was happening and telling our pandemic stories. As the pandemic wore on, we discussed the shifts we saw. Around the world, people's mental health was negatively affected. Clients shared feelings of increased anxiety and depression, difficulty sleeping, and stress about isolation and the possibility of job loss. They were also experiencing decision-making fatigue.

Many people began losing their jobs or contemplating significant life changes. It became known as the Great Resignation. People claimed to flee their circumstances because the pandemic shifted their perspectives.

Success *and* Significance

Significance is the quality of being worthy of attention. I believe the deeper shift happening is about meaning and significance. It is a longing to be a part of something greater than ourselves—to have belongingness.

What is *really* worthy of our attention? *What matters?*

More of us are realizing we want to live and work differently. We want to balance material markers of success with what matters most. We want to feel more in balance.

We are learning how to do it. Internal and external shifts are happening at a pace we haven't experienced before. We are feeling emotionally unsettled. Our nervous systems are on overdrive. Many stories are coming at us from different channels telling us what to believe about ourselves, others, and our world. Where we focus our attention matters.

Beliefs

Like the food we eat, the information we consume begins to shape us and our actions. Ways of thinking become our beliefs. They influence how we feel about ourselves and others. They limit and expand our choices.

Examples of beliefs that can affect motivation and actions:

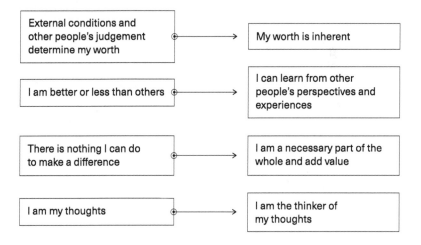

Limiting Beliefs	Expanding Beliefs
External conditions and other people's judgement determine my worth	My worth is inherent
I am better or less than others	I can learn from other people's perspectives and experiences
There is nothing I can do to make a difference	I am a necessary part of the whole and add value
I am my thoughts	I am the thinker of my thoughts

We move between two levels of existence: the individual and collective. These narratives create our collective future. How do we unpack our narratives and be open to new ones?

Remembering You Are Not Your Thoughts

After his release from 28 years in prison, Nelson Mandela boarded a plane and noticed a Black African at the controls. What surprised him was his fear and nervousness. How could the anti-apartheid revolutionary have internalized a negative stereotype about Black incompetence? He had spent most of his life fighting against what he was now experiencing inside himself.[2]

This is how we evolve individually and collectively. We open ourselves and remain curious about what might be lying hidden and unconscious. We all have biases and habitual ways of thinking. We assume the story we are telling about ourselves and others is true. Few beliefs will prove to be true for all people in all circumstances. We are learning what is true for us through our life experiences.

It is easy to believe you are your thoughts. We attach our identity to our beliefs. This happens with politics, religion, economics, and other ideological systems. Many times we are just downloading old thought patterns. We forget to question the effect these narratives have on our minds, hearts, and shaping reality.

Thoughts come and go. They are like the ticker constantly running on news channels. These outlets cycle the same news over and over again. It is easy to forget we are reading them as they pass by. Yet, we can consciously choose which news stories to pay attention to and which ones to let go of. It is the same with thoughts.

Refining Our Minds

We offer ourselves and others compassion by remembering we can change our minds anytime, choose a different thought or position, and reposition our attention. We can remember that the more we defend a belief, the more we will live that belief out. Take a moment to consider which beliefs you want to live out? Which beliefs do we want future generations to live out?

Some ideas cause great harm to others and lead to suffering. What do we do in the face of so much pain and harm?

Negativity and harmful language or actions from another do not justify responding in kind. We can exercise accountability with compassion instead of having a vengeful heart. We can begin by taking personal responsibility for the thoughts we choose to speak and bring into reality. It is a reminder to use our personal power and passion wisely.

Understanding the Brain and Thought

Our brains are wired for negativity, and human beings tend to have beliefs and emotions that can harm themselves and others. When overwhelmed and stressed, our brains' higher-order "executive functions" effectively shut down. We revert to operating from the more primitive and reactive brain centers, which explains our tendency for defensiveness. We get attached to being right and when our beliefs are challenged it threatens our identity.[3] To cope, we unconsciously repeat patterns of behavior to protect ourselves based on fear and insecurity. This is the fight or flight response. When we are feeling negative and need to shift, can we stop and remember what matters most?

We have made significant progress in understanding ways to increase mental fitness. Neuroplasticity is a process where we train our brains and build new neural pathways. Examples of behaviors that encourage neuroplasticity are learning a new language, memory tasks and games, yoga, exercise, and mindfulness. Research shows us that in as little as two weeks of disciplined mindfulness practice, there are measurable changes in the number of connections between neurons and in the thickness of the brain's areas connected to self-awareness, greater self-mastery, and higher mental processing.[4] We only realize these potentials if we have the discipline to engage in the inner work to develop new neural pathways in the brain.

Shifting Your Perspective

One of the tools we use in coaching is reframing. In a recent call with a client, she described how terrible one of her employee's behaviors was. She was highly triggered, and her frustration was palpable.

We explored her assumptions about this employee and how these beliefs led her to behave. When I asked her a reframing question, "What would the employee say about what is happening if he was here?" She stopped speaking and thought for a moment. She revealed that he would be surprised to hear she wasn't happy with his performance. She hadn't yet considered his perspective and what was happening from his point of view.

To Reframe Your Thinking, Ask Yourself:

What are my assumptions?

What is the impact on my behavior and actions? The relationship?

What is another way of thinking about this?

What would the other person involved have to say about this situation?

Understanding Energy and Emotions

The way you think also impacts your energy level. It affects how you feel about yourself and others. It contributes to your emotional state and the state of others.

I like to define emotions as energies in motion. E-motions. We each have different energies flowing through us, and they are contagious. Have you ever been around someone who is high energy? They speak with joy, optimism, and hope. You leave this conversation feeling lighter and with positive expectations. They transferred their expansive energy to you. The same happens with the heavier energies that keep us stuck.

In *Ask and It Is Given*, the authors introduce an Emotional Guidance Scale.[5] A scale of your range of emotions looks like this:

Expansive energies are numbers 1–7. Transitional energies, which can be liberating or limiting, are numbers 8–16. Limiting and constricting energies are numbers 17–22. None of these energies are wrong. What is important to remember is that you cannot deny energy, you can experience it and transform it.

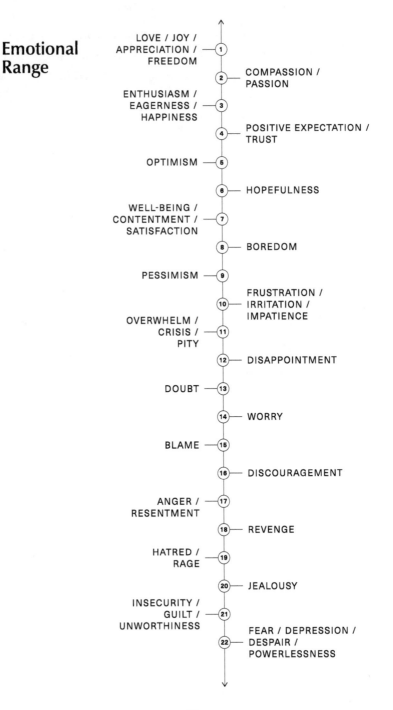

Emotional Range

1 — LOVE / JOY / APPRECIATION / FREEDOM

2 — COMPASSION / PASSION

3 — ENTHUSIASM / EAGERNESS / HAPPINESS

4 — POSITIVE EXPECTATION / TRUST

5 — OPTIMISM

6 — HOPEFULNESS

7 — WELL-BEING / CONTENTMENT / SATISFACTION

8 — BOREDOM

9 — PESSIMISM

10 — FRUSTRATION / IRRITATION / IMPATIENCE

11 — OVERWHELM / CRISIS / PITY

12 — DISAPPOINTMENT

13 — DOUBT

14 — WORRY

15 — BLAME

16 — DISCOURAGEMENT

17 — ANGER / RESENTMENT

18 — REVENGE

19 — HATRED / RAGE

20 — JEALOUSY

21 — INSECURITY / GUILT / UNWORTHINESS

22 — FEAR / DEPRESSION / DESPAIR / POWERLESSNESS

Authentic Emotion

Many of us have learned to present with false emotions and pretend we are in a state we are not. Acceptance of authentic emotion opens the door to transition. This is why talking about our experiences honestly and expressing emotion can be very healing. It moves the energy.

Learning to work with and shift your energy consciously is at the heart of creating a meaningful life. Your emotions gauge what feels good and right for you and help guide you to a more loving and empowering style of living.

I recently took two weeks off from work and completely disconnected from email. Normally after a few weeks off, I come back feeling happy and eager to serve my clients. When I returned from vacation, I noticed I was feeling frustrated and discouraged. These feelings were starting to affect my other relationships. While I wanted to pretend I was satisfied and content after a two-week vacation, I was deceiving myself. This was a display of false emotion.

With some deeper reflection and a few coaching conversations with wise colleagues, I expressed my frustration and discouragement and made some decisions about my priorities. I decided to let go of some work. I shared this change with clients and authentic emotions of well-being, appreciation, and joy emerged again.

My life didn't change significantly. My experience of my life changed.

Shifting to Higher Levels of Energy Collectively

Meaning is the sister of experience, and to discern the meaning of what has happened to you is one of the essential ways of finding your inner belonging and discovering the sheltering presence of your soul.

John O'Donohue[6]

Imagine a world where more of us believe our value is inherent. You have a sense of belonging and trust life's inherent value. You see others as creative and worthy. You are open and are learning from their experiences. You take responsibility for your words and actions. You consider how they impact others. You have greater clarity on what is most important to you and how you want to spend your energy and time. You know how you find significance and can share this with others. You believe you have strengths and skills that make a difference. You are using your power with others in service of the greater good.

With these thoughts, you spend more time in expansive energies. You feel more appreciation, joy, and hopefulness. This is a place of resonance. You experience more meaningfulness and significance.

Changemakers, coaches, conscious leadership consultants, teachers, and other professionals doing transformational work— are helping people to be better human beings. We are letting go of narratives that keep us in the same patterns. When we know better, we do better.

Choice Is the Process of Creation Itself

You cannot control all of life's circumstances. The creation process is about trusting life and choosing based on resonance. This means you don't have to see what the future will look like. You can choose to find significance through your challenges, work, and love.

Your current choices are a reflection of the future you are creating. Positive expectation is anticipating that life is working in your favor. If you want a future that is full of meaning and joy, you can choose to cultivate more meaning and joy now. The change process is the dance of deep acceptance and appreciation of how things are now and a willingness to pursue a desired future.

Creating a Sustainable Future for All

No matter what sort of difficulties, how painful the experience is, if we lose our hope, that's our real disaster.
Dalai Lama XIV

If we lose hope, we have lost our way. We can choose to remember who we are and our responsibility to future generations. We can make choices and decisions that demonstrate humility, compassion, and ethics. We can find a way to listen to one another. We can soften our hearts and seek to make sense of what is happening in a loving and empowering way that opens a door for us to embrace one another. We can find our way to meaningfulness through the mess. How we make meaning is deeply personal and unique as each of our lives is a multitude of experiences and variables. Most of us are given a blueprint from our families and cultures of origin about belonging and how to assess our value or worth. Stories are shared between generations about what matters most and the elements of a life well-lived.

At some point in our lives, we will experience a disorienting event that causes us to question our deeply ingrained patterns, beliefs, and assumptions. Joseph Campbell describes this pattern as departure, initiation, and return or the inner journey. Telling our stories is how we bring meaning to our experiences and become more conscious of our lives and social impact.

For many of us, the pandemic was our disorientation. It took us back to our homes. It took us to stillness, contemplation and deep thinking, stress and longing. It was our pause so we could come back to what was meaningful and pay attention to what matters most.

Epilogue

We either own our stories or they own us. Only when we have the courage to own our history are we able to write a brave new ending to our story. This is true in our lives, our families, our communities, and our country.
Brené Brown

Y(our) Story Is Still Being Written

I received my first book on coaching as a birthday present from my mom. It was a book by Patrick Williams and Diane S. Menendez called *Becoming a Professional Life Coach* (2007). I read the first few chapters and decided I needed to hire a coach before becoming one. I learned a lot. Over a decade later, I received the Master Certified Coach credential from the International Coaching Federation. I still consistently seek the guidance of a personal coach, and I invest in ongoing learning and development to grow my capabilities and capacity to serve.

I enrolled in a course on transformative presence this year. Dr. Pat Williams, the author of the book, is in my cohort. We set up a call to connect outside of the group recently. I pulled his book off the shelf to show him. The book opened to the page where I noted my original tagline for Imprint: *y(our) story is still being written*. I noticed all of the parts I had underlined and decided to reread these first couple of chapters. They cite Alfred Adler's work on significance and belonging.

Alfred Adler was a student of Maria Montessori who believed the primary need of every student is a sense of belonging and significance. The Montessori program emphasized a positive sense of self and a duty to contribute to a community, leading to a greater sense of meaning and connection. As adults, in an accelerated environment with social norms quickly dissolving, we would be wise to revisit how to be competent in our communities. What are our expectations of one another? How can we cultivate respect, grace, and courtesy in the social order? This is our call to write our brave new ending amidst the mess. Meaning and happiness happen in community and in relationships.

I shared with Pat that one of the most important learnings during my creative process was listening to and trusting my intuition. I told him I wanted to reframe the conversation on meaning. I didn't know what that would look like though. I began researching meaning and found evidence to support my instincts about significance. I discovered the four dimensions of meaning, confirming I was on the right track.

I am learning to stay with ideas long enough to do the deep work and make connections. I am lighter for having owned my story and history. I learned to stay with an idea and to follow the threads of inspiration and curiosity.

I have also realized there is tension between my desire for happiness and my desire for a meaningful life. I want to find personal meaning. When I wrote we are in a crisis for meaning, I didn't understand the predictors of happiness versus the predictors of meaningfulness. This is a tension that won't ever be solved, resolved, or fixed. It is an ongoing invitation to be in relationship with my life energy, examining my life, and creating internal and external balance.

I read recently that the first college degree in happiness is now being offered. As Frankl wisely advised, happiness cannot be pursued but must ensue. Predictors of happiness include satisfying basic desires, being in good health, having financial well-being, focusing on the present, and being the recipient of people's generosity. Yet, disorienting events disrupt, or we ourselves disrupt, this equilibrium in search of something more meaningful. Meaningfulness comes from reflecting on our struggles and challenges, deep thought, experiencing stress, thinking about the future and past, and doing things for others.

What makes me happy may not make life meaningful, and what makes life meaningful may not make me happy. I am finding a middle way. Holding the individual and the collective and the material and physical. Recognizing the upsides and downsides of overvaluing one and diminishing the other.

One of the other joys of this process was my late father-in-law, Mickey Hollingshead. He agreed to be one of the interviewees for the pilot after he was diagnosed with pancreatic cancer. I wondered what he would share while facing his mortality. His primary indicator was Challenge, and his secondary was Love. The desire to share more of his life story grew from this first structured interview. We decided to record a series of Zoom calls with his wife, Andi, where he talked through his life history. I watched him come alive as I witnessed him. We spent hours together, and then ultimately transcribed the stories, refined and fact checked them with family, and then created a personal history book to share at our Hollingshead Family Reunion in July, 2021. He walked into the library and read a few excerpts from his history, beginning with his legacy. He read, "My legacy would be being a good person. I don't have any aspirations to be on the top of the map. Just to be a good husband, a good parent, a good son. I hope that what I transmit is a good family." This is the same message he would share with us, specifically Addison and Jack, as he sensed he wasn't going to be with us much longer. He reminded them to be good people above all, and this is about how you treat people and honor everyone. He cautioned us not to let material things take over our humanity.

Mickey navigated the last year of his life with wisdom and love. I felt like I had a masterclass in how to transition from this realm to the next. When I first learned of his diagnosis, and we got on the phone together, I was surprised when he first said to me, "Michelle, I've had a great life." He was genuinely filled with gratitude and appreciation for his relationships and experiences. He planned to enjoy the remaining time he had on his terms.

I was so touched by his celebration of life and the seven-minute video he recorded to show at his service. He began the video with a twinkle in his eye, looked at us and said, "I bet you all are wondering why I have called you all here today." Then he started to laugh. Once again, he expressed appreciation for a life well-lived, his experiences, and his most important relationships—personal and professional. Mickey wrote a brave ending.

What matters in the end is also what matters in the middle and today. What can you give? How can you accompany others to find and feel greater significance? This is the antidote to our collective crisis for meaning.

About the Author

Michelle Hollingshead specializes in transformational change. She is an entrepreneur, an author, and an International Coach Federation Master Certified Coach. She is the founder of Imprint, a coaching and consulting company and is part of a global community committed to developing conscious leaders and organizations. Her clients include Fortune 500 companies, privately-held companies, and non-profits. As an expert in integral leadership development and corporate culture transformation, she works with diverse backgrounds to co-create community and realize potential. Michelle holds a Master of Education from Lesley University and has extensive training in yoga, meditation, mindfulness, and various diagnostic tools. She is a proud mother of two and lives in Lexington, Kentucky, with her husband, Dan.

References

Chapter 1

1. Cherry, Kendra, "How to Recognize and Cope with an Identity Crisis, Very Well Mind, April 11, 2023, https://www.verywellmind.com/what-is-an-identity-crisis-2795948#:~:text=An%20identity%20crisis%20is%20a%20developmental%20event%20that,of%20the%20most%20important%20conflicts%20that%20people%20face.

2. Twenge, et. al., "Age, Period, and Cohort Trends in Mood Disorder Indicators and Suicide Related Outcomes in a Nationally Representative Dataset, 2005–2017," *Journal of Abnormal Psychology* Vol. 128, No. 3 (2019), 185–99, cites the following findings, "Since the late 2000s, the mental health of teens and young adults in the U.S. has declined dramatically.... Between 2009 and 2017, rates of depression among kids ages 14 to 17 increased by more than 60%. The increases were nearly as steep among those ages 12 to 13 (47%) and 18 to 21 (46%), and rates roughly doubled among those ages 20 to 21. In 2017—the latest year for which federal data are available—more than one in eight Americans ages 12 to 25 experienced a major depressive episode."
The same trends held when the researchers analyzed the data on suicides, attempted suicides and "serious psychological distress"—a term applied to people who score high on a test that measures feelings of sadness, nervousness and hopelessness. Among young people, rates of suicidal thoughts, plans and attempts all increased significantly, and in some cases more than doubled, between 2008 and 2017, the study found.

3. The American Psychiatric Association published the following statistics in 2019, "The suicide rate increased 33 percent from 1999 through 2017, from 10.5 to 14 suicides per

100,000 people (Hedegaard, MD, et. al., "Suicide Mortality in the United States, 1999–2017," NCHS Data Brief No. 330, November 2018). Rates have increased more sharply since 2006. Suicide ranks as the fourth leading cause of death for people ages 35 to 54, and the second for 10- to 34-year-olds. It remains the tenth leading cause of death overall. But it's a different story in other parts of the world. Over roughly the same period, other countries have seen rates fall, including Japan, China, Russia and most of Western Europe. And while the climbing rates are cause for concern, experts point out that they don't tell the whole story. In fact, the U.S. suicide rate is similar today to the rate of 30 years ago. Deaths by suicide fell markedly in the 1980s and 1990s before rising again at the turn of the century. What's more, while some countries, such as Russia, have seen dramatic declines in suicide rates since the 1990s, their rates are still well above those in the United States.

In other words, there is no obvious culprit for an increase in suicides — nor is there a single, easy solution we can import from other nations to turn the trend around. Yet there are clues.

Socioeconomic changes might be part of the puzzle. Globally, suicide rates have often fallen when living conditions have improved. And the reverse is also true. Princeton University economists Anne Case, PhD, and Angus Deaton, PhD, have shown that deaths from suicide, drugs and alcohol have risen steeply among white, middle-aged Americans since 2000 ("Rising morbidity and mortality in midlife among white non-Hispanic Americans in the 21st century," PNAS, Vol. 112, No. 49, 2015). They also argue these "deaths of despair" are linked to a deterioration of economic and social well-being among the white working class (Mortality and Morbidity in the 21st Century, Brookings Papers on Economic Activity, Spring 2017)."

4. Pew Research Center, Oct. 17, 2019, "In U.S., Decline of Christianity Continues at Rapid Pace."

5. Costin, et. al., "Meaning is about mattering: Evaluating coherence, purpose, and existential mattering as precursors of meaning in life judgments," *J Pers Soc Psychol*, April 2020. Existential mattering (henceforth, mattering, George & Park, 2014; also known as "significance": Martela & Steger, 2016), describes experiences of value, worth, and transcending "the trivial or momentary" conditions of our lives (George & Park, 2016; Heintzelman & King, 2014b; King et al., 2006). In having a sense of mattering, one feels that one's actions make a difference in the world and that life is worth living (George & Park, 2016; Martela & Steger, 2016). Although mattering has received much less empirical attention compared with the other two dimensions (George & Park, 2014).

6. Thus, when deciding whether their life is meaningful or not, people seem to ask whether their life matters despite their smallness in time (Homo sapiens have existed for more than 200,000 years, and the Universe has existed for more than 13.73 billion years) and space (the vastness of the Universe). This finding held across gender, wealth, political orientation, relationship status, religion, and lower or higher overall meaningfulness. Thus, the link from mattering to MIL judgments seemingly holds regardless of whether one's life is seen to matter in a spiritual sense (e.g., by being God's creation) or in a secular sense (e.g., mattering to important others or to future generations), and regardless of whether one's life is seen as more or less meaningful. Costin, et. al., "Meaning is about mattering: Evaluating coherence, purpose, and existential mattering as precursors of meaning in life judgments," *J Pers Soc Psychol*, April 2020.

7. Experiencing one's life as meaningful is associated with measurable benefits. Self-reported meaning in life (MIL) has been linked to healthier eating, more physical activity, higher life satisfaction, and lower depression. Hooker, et. al., "A Meaningful Life is a Healthy Life: A Conceptual Model Linking Meaning and Meaning Salience to Health," *Review of General Psychology*, Vol. 22, Issue 1 (2018), 11–24.

8. Martela, et. al., "The three meanings of meaning in life: Distinguishing coherence, purpose, and significance," *Journal of Positive Psychology*, Vol. 11, Issue 5 (2015), 531–45.

9. Our results therefore support calls to supplement the emphasis on coherence or purpose in the psychological literature on meaning with a much stronger focus on understanding how people come to develop and maintain a sense of mattering in their lives, and the consequences of doing so or otherwise.
   Heine, et. al., "The meaning maintenance model: On the coherence of social motivations," *Personality and Social Psychology Review*, Vol. 10, Issue 2 (2006), 88–110.
   McKnight, et. al., "Purpose in life as a system that creates and sustains health and well-being: An integrative, testable theory," *Review of General Psychology*, Vol. 13, (2009), 242–51
   Costin, et. al., "Meaning is about mattering: Evaluating coherence, purpose, and existential mattering as precursors of meaning in life judgments," *J Pers Soc Psychol*, April 2020.

10. Generativity (i.e., "the concern in establishing and guiding the next generation"; Erikson, 1963, p. 267) carries the sense that one's life matters for something. Highly generative individuals are more likely to construct stories that involve awareness of the suffering of others, redeeming bad situations into good outcomes, and committing to goals that benefit others. McAdams, et. al., "Generativity, the Big Five, and Psychosocial Adaptation in Midlife Adults," *Journal of Personality*, Vol. 78, No. 4 (Aug. 2010).

Chapter 2

1. Greater purpose in life predicted faster recovery from a negative emotional stimulus, suggesting that purpose may be related to more adaptive regulation of negative emotions. Hooker, et. al., "A meaningful life is a healthy life: A conceptual model linking meaning and meaning salience to health," *Review of General Psychology*, Vol.22, Issue 1 (2018).
2. Fortgang, *Now What?: 90 Days to a New Life Direction* (New York: TarcherPerigree, 2015).
3. Laloux, *Reinventing Organizations: A Guide to Creating Organizations Inspired by the Next Stage in Human Consciousness* (Brussels: Nelson Parker, 2014).
4. Kofman, *Conscious Business: How to Build Value through Values* (Louisville: Sounds True, 2013).

Chapter 3

1. Gates, et. al., *Meditations from the Mat: Daily Reflections on the Path of Yoga* (New York: Anchor, 2002).
2. Winfrey, Oprah. "Super Soul." *Super Soul Special: Oprah and Eckhart Tolle: Acceptance of Troubled Times.* February 9, 2022.

Chapter 4

1. Hooker, et. al., "A meaningful life is a healthy life: A conceptual model linking meaning and meaning salience to health," *Review of General Psychology*, Vol.22, Issue 1 (2018).
2. Carstensen, et. al., "Emotional Experience Improves with Age: Evidence Based on over 10 years of Experience Sampling," *Psychology and Aging*, Vol. 26 (2011): 21–33.
3. Carstensen, et. al., "Goals Change when Life's Fragility Is Primed: Lessons Learned from Older Adults, the September 11 Attacks and SARS," *Social Cognition*, Vol. 24 (2006): 248–78.
4. Gawande, *Being Mortal: Medicine and What Matters in the End* (London: Profile Books, 2014).

5. Brooks, *Mormonism and White Supremacy: American Religion and the Problem of Racial Innocence* (Oxford: Oxford University Press, 2020).

Chapter 5

1. "One third of your life is spent at work," https://www.gettysburg.edu/news/stories?id=79db7b34-630c-4f49-ad32-4ab9ea48e72b.

2. Chamine, *Positive Intelligence: Why Only 20% of Teams and Individuals Achieve Their True Potential and How You Can Achieve Yours* (Austin: Greenleaf, 2012).

3. Taylor, *Walking the Talk: Building a Culture for Success* (London: Cornerstone, 2015).

4. "What is a B Corporation: Everything You Need to Know, "https://www.cultivatingcapital.com/b-corporation/#:~:text=B%20Corporations%2C%20commonly%20known%20as%20B%20Corps%2C%20are,of%20business%20to%20address%20social%20and%20environmental%20problems.

5. "What Google Learned from Its Quest to Build the Perfect Team," *New York Times*, 26 Feb. 2016.

6. Lahey, et. al., *An Everyone Culture: Becoming a Deliberately Developmental Organization* (Boston: Harvard Business Review, 2016).

7. Busse. et. al., "Toward a 'Meaningful Self' at the Workplace: Multinational Evidence from Asia, Europe, and North America," *Journal of Leadership and Organizational Studies* Vol. 25, Issue 1 (2018).

8. Bailey, et. al., "What Makes Work Meaningful—or Meaningless," *MIT Sloan Management Review*, 1 June, 2016.

Chapter 6

1. Oliver, *The Self Delusion: The Surprising Science of Our Connection to Each Other and the Natural World* (London:Weidenfeld & Nicolson, 2021).
2. Adams, et. al., "Promoting Self-Compassionate Attitudes Toward Eating Among Restrictive and Guilty Eaters," *Journal of Social and Clinical Psychology*, Vol. 26, No. 10, (2007), pp. 1120–1144.
3. Scott, *Radical Candor: Be a Kick-Ass Boss Without Losing Your Humanity* (Revised, Updated) (Manhattan: St. Martin's, 2019).
4. McAdams, et. al., "A theory of generativity and its assessment self-report, behavioral acts, and narrative themes in autobiography," *Journal of Personality and Social Psychology*, Vol. 62 (1992), 221–30.

Chapter 7

1. Danly, www.lezadanly.com
2. Mandela, *A Long Walk to Freedom: The Autobiography of Nelson Mandela* (Manhattan: Time Warner, 1995).
3. Breaking Bias NeuroLeadership Journal Volume 5 May 2014 Matthew D. Lieberman, David Rock and Christine L. Coxscience.
4. Levey, et. al., *Mindfulness, Meditation, and Mind Fitness: (Spiritual Fitness, Mindset, Focus, Stress-Reduction)* (Newburyport: Conari, 2015).
5. Hicks, et. al., *Ask and It Is Given: Learning to Manifest Your Desires* (Carlsbad: Hay House, 2004).
6. O'Donohue, *Anam Cara: A Book of Celtic Wisdom* (NYC: Harper Collins, 1998).

**CHANGEMAKERS
BOOKS**

Transform your life, transform our world. Changemakers
Books publishes books for people who seek to become positive,
powerful agents of change. These books inform, inspire, and
provide practical wisdom and skills to empower us to write
the next chapter of humanity's future.
www.changemakers-books.com

Current Bestsellers from Changemakers Books

Resetting our Future: Am I Too Old to Save the Planet?
A Boomer's Guide to Climate Action
Lawrence MacDonald

Why American boomers are uniquely responsible for the
climate crisis — and what to do about it.

Resetting our Future: Feeding Each Other
Shaping Change in Food Systems through Relationship
Michelle Auerbach and Nicole Civita

Our collective survival depends on making food systems more
relational; this guidebook for shaping change in food systems
offers a way to find both security and pleasure in a more
connected, well-nourished life.

Resetting Our Future: Zero Waste Living, The 80/20 Way
The Busy Person's Guide to a Lighter Footprint
Stephanie J. Miller

Empowering the busy individual to do the easy things that
have a real impact on the climate and waste crises.

The Way of the Rabbit
Mark Hawthorne

An immersion in the world of rabbits: their habitats, evolution
and biology; their role in legend, literature, and popular
culture; and their significance as household companions.